My View From Seven Feet

In Paintings & Narratives

JOE BARRY CARROLL

Joe Barry Carroll Publishing

Atlanta, GA

Joe Barry Carroll Publishing
Atlanta, Georgia
joebarrycarrollpublishing.com

ISBN-13: 978-1-7332144-0-7 (paperback)
Library of Congress Control Number: 2019910571

The paper used in this publication meets the minimum requirements of the American National Standard for Information Sciences—permanence of paper for printed library materials ANSI Z39.48-1992

CONTENTS

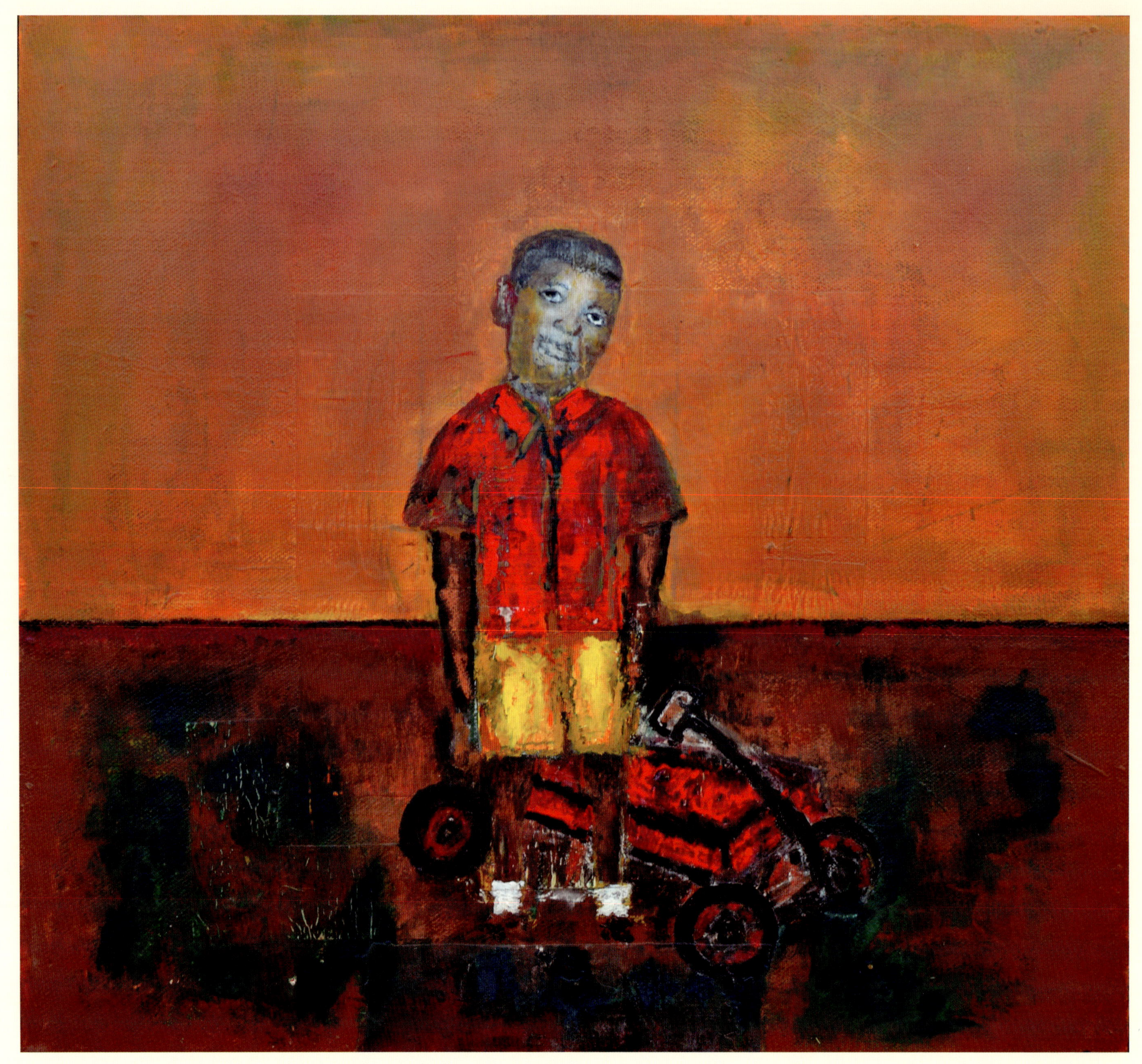

WAGON

Acrylic and mixed materials on board
48" x 48"

A BOY'S LESSON

Neither of my parents tolerated very much mischief, especially my mother. I recall being intercepted by Momma as I made my way through the back door of our house there at 611 East Harding Street. She was disturbed by some silly thing I had done, as many boys have while testing the boundaries of their youth. Her instruction to me, while restraining herself from placing hands on me, still rings in my ears all these years later.

Son, I need us to be clear. It is more important for me to be your mother than your playmate. If you need someone to play patty-cake with, I recommend you go over there to the playground and find someone in the sandbox for that, because I am not the one. Loving my children and spoiling them can never be the same thing. My responsibility is to prepare you for most of what the world is about to hand you. None of that preparation includes allowing you to take shortcuts and try to be slick. Every shortcut that I know about leads to a dead-end, and being slick is likely to slide you right into trouble. You are going to be an adult one day, and I am not going to have the world pointing a finger and blaming me for allowing one of my boys to grow into a sorry-ass man. The world has enough of the sorry kind, and I refuse to participate in adding another one to the population. It just ain't going to happen with my children, not if I can help it.

In memory of Annie Mae Carroll (1925-2012)

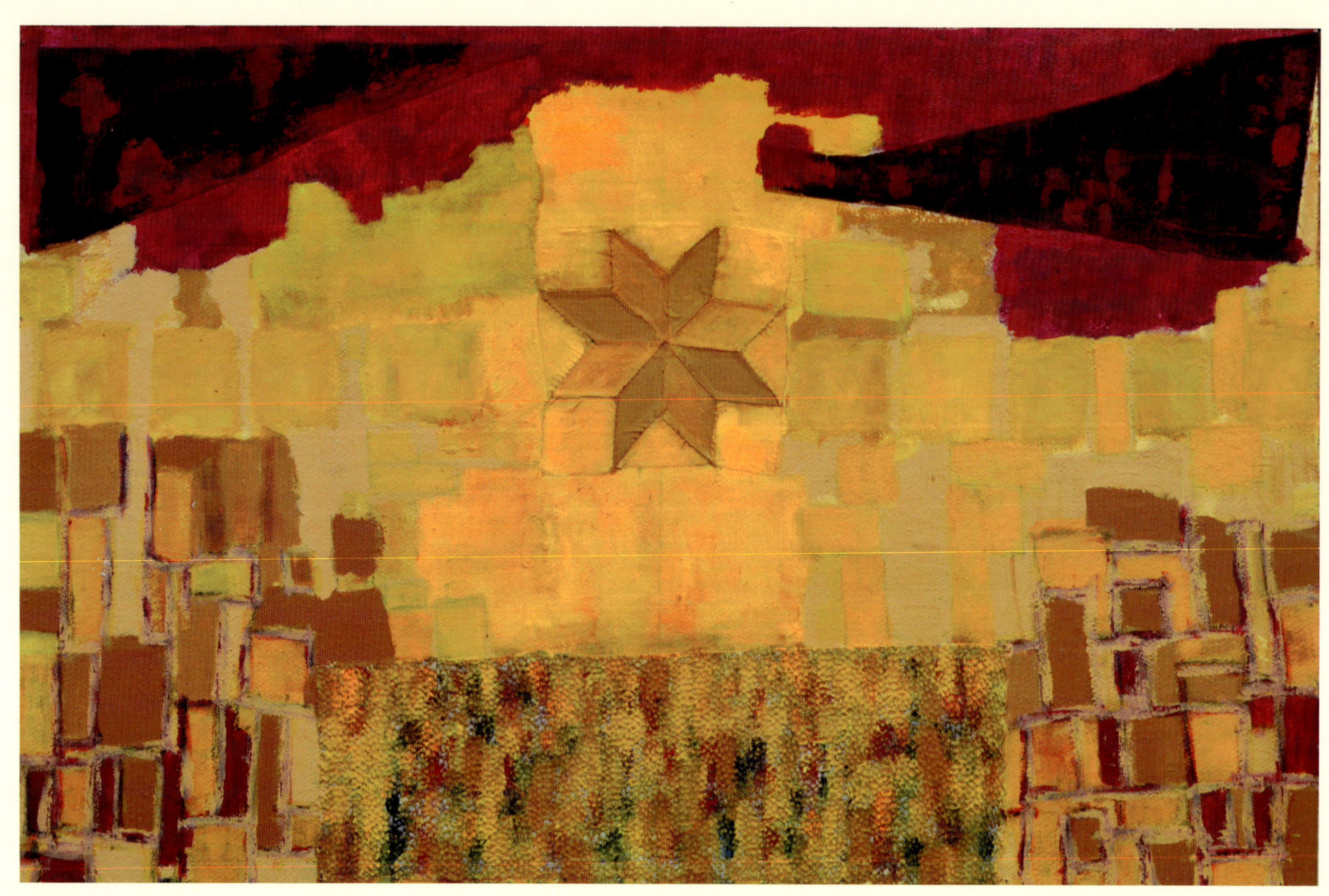

STAR

Acrylic and mixed materials on board
48" x 32"

STARS

Sometimes, delving into a celebrity's backstory is like visiting the back kitchen at your favorite restaurant—you may not want to see the details of just how the sausage is made. We seem to have an unrealistic expectation of athletes, entertainers, and rock stars, resulting in an unrealistic estimation of who they are or could be beyond their specific talents that entertain us. We become heartbroken when yet another of our stars falls from the sky on the heels of scandal and other unpleasant revelations. Who and what a person is when they are unknown is likely to follow them into celebrity and stardom. Their humanity does not necessarily evolve because they run fast, jump high, or sing well. The reality is that our celebrities are likely to be flawed; some are more flawed than others. Not necessarily in a horrible way, but in the way every human is flawed. Perhaps we should be satisfied with the wonderful gift of song, sport, or anything else that stars provide their fans, and leave it there.

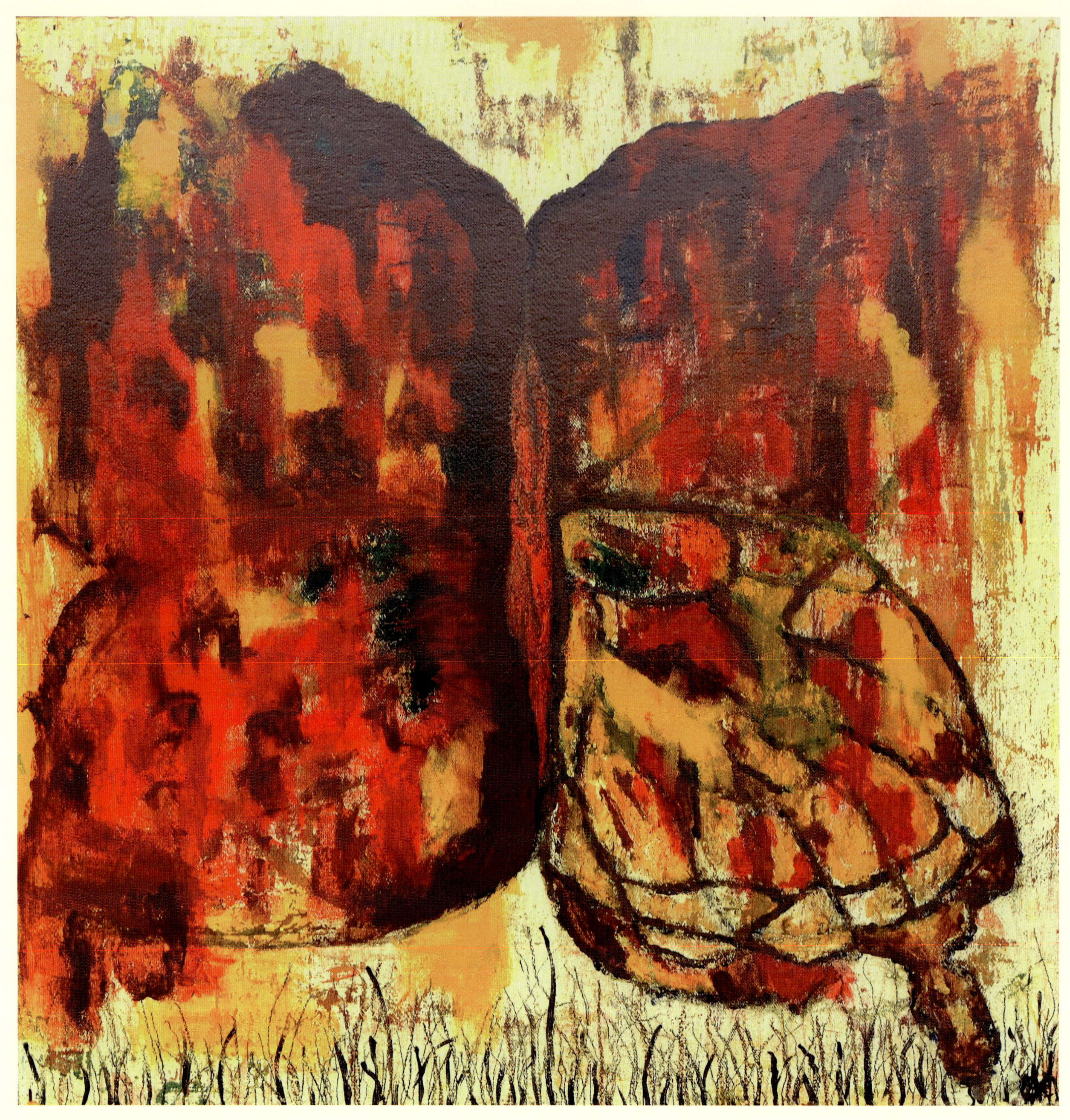

FLY

Acrylic on board
48" x 48"

A DISCOVERY

No matter how much I know and experience, there will always be something new to discover. I expect that to be true for the remainder of my life. I believe it is this way for most of us, especially if we remain open to the new, the unknown, and the possible.

My eleven years of professional basketball have been followed by thirty years of serving as an investment portfolio advisor for wealthy families. Then, a few years ago, I jumped into the deep end of the art pool without any formal training or direction. Over the years, I have visited art galleries and museums throughout the world as a patron and enthusiast but never considered myself an artist. Each journey into my canvas continues to be a revelation.

My artwork now lives alongside my investment advisory practice and my writing. I offer my journey, so far, as a testament to what may lie within each of us. There may be many new things waiting to be discovered, whether that be art, writing a book, traveling to a distant place, starting a new career, or whatever lies on the spectrum of our human potential.

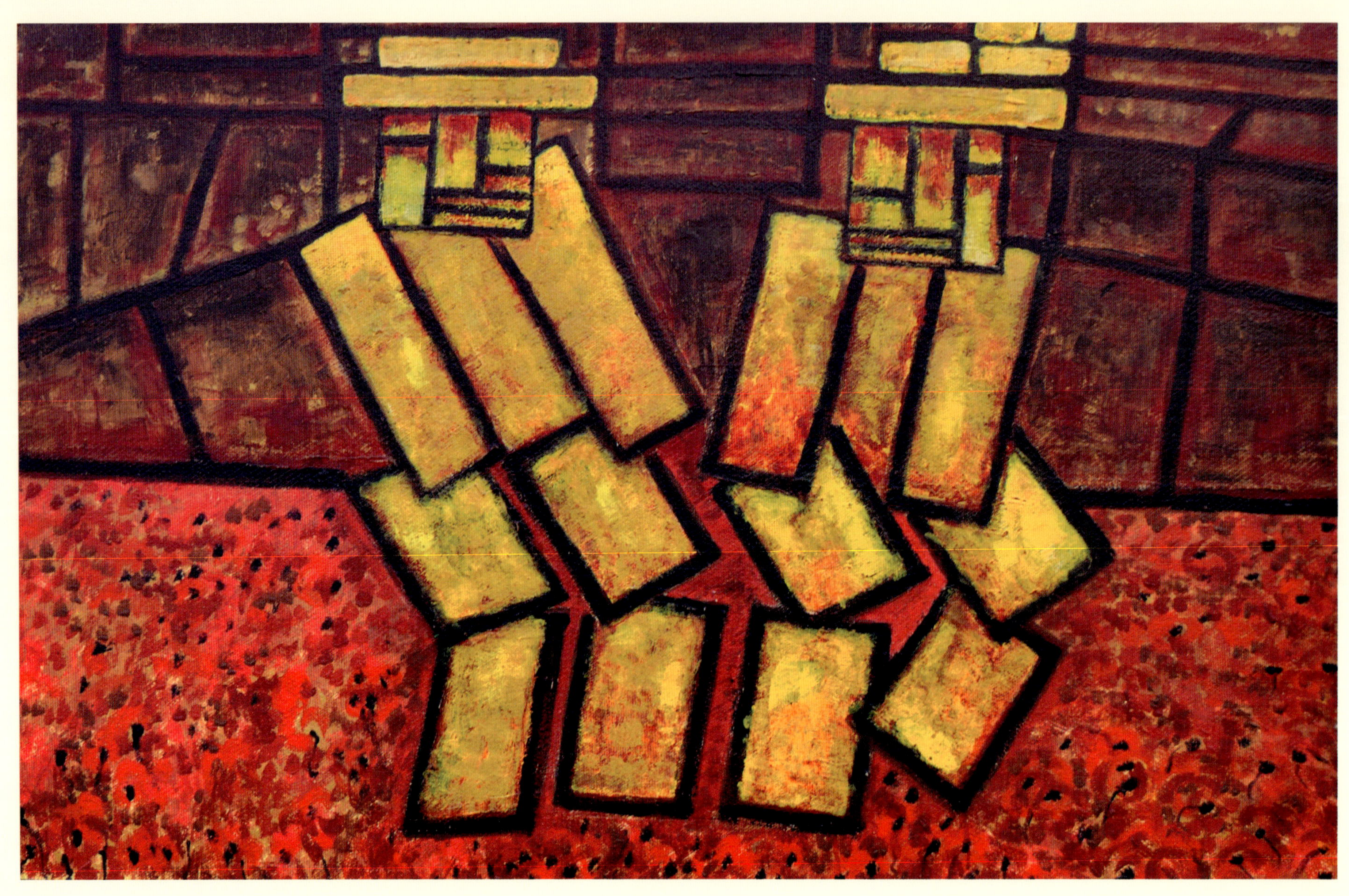

BOOGIE

Acrylic on board
48" x 32"

MUTUALITY

Whether business or personal, great relationships are built on an exchange of *value* and *values*. I am reminded of the conversation my friend shared with me that he had with one of his young-adult children. His child was clear-eyed and adamant in her requirement of someone with this much money, that much education, a certain kind of appearance, and so on. He in reply said that yes, those are all good requirements, and that he understood the benefit of what she was seeking. Furthermore, he wanted all of that and more for his pride and only daughter. However, he went on to inquire as to what she would provide in return. On the surface, his query was most likely one of those awkward daddy-daughter exchanges when a father chides his child, but the lesson that lay beneath is a takeaway for any of us. Great relationships occur when each party contributes something of value to the other person. Each party may be contributing something different in form, but not in substance and weight. Part of our journey in relationship with another person is bound up in this discovery. We would be wise to ask ourselves what contribution we bring to the relationships we seek.

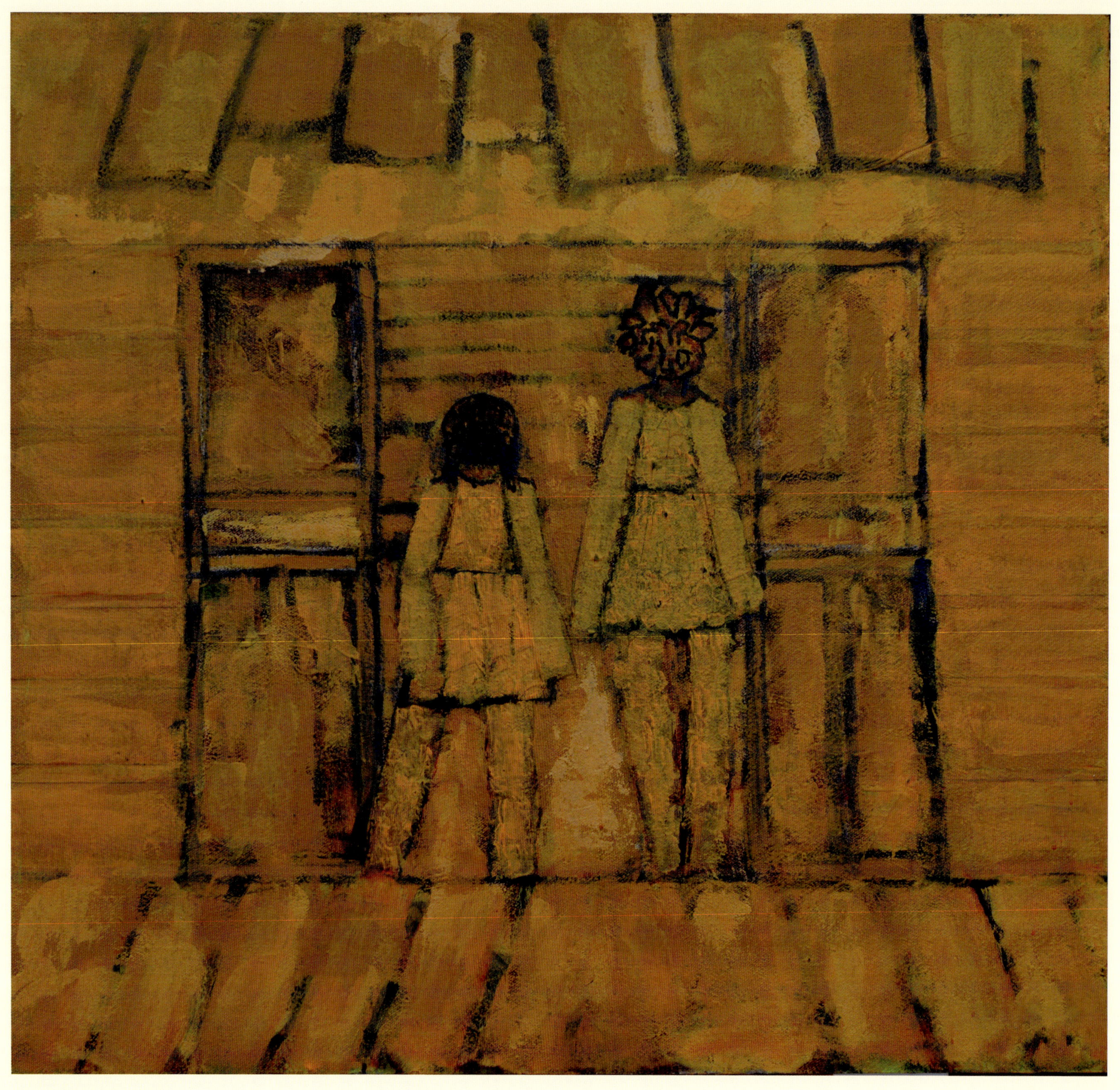

TWO

Acrylic on board
48" x 48"

We learn as we live…

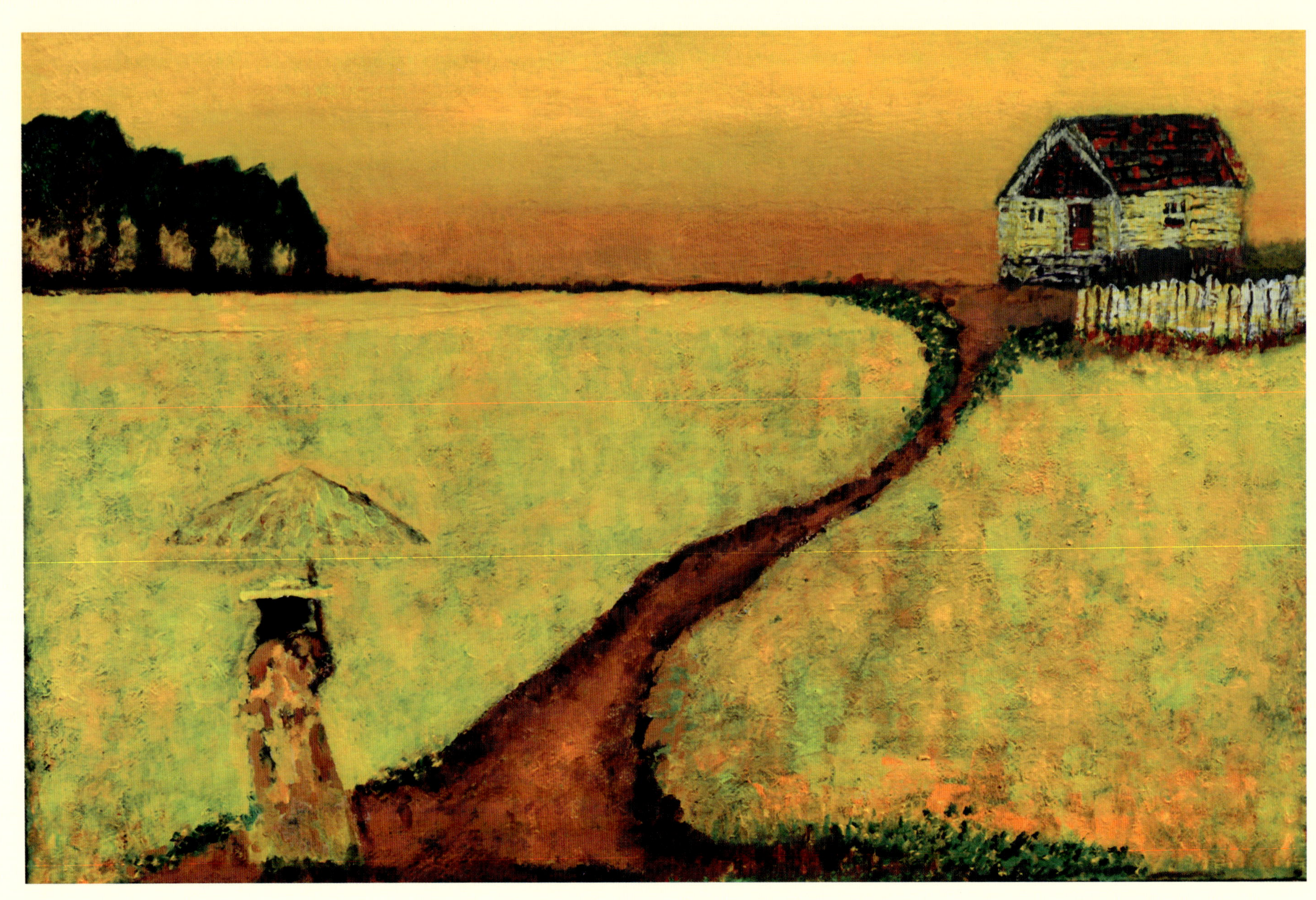

SUMMA

Acrylic on board
48" x 32"

NOSTALGIA

Can it be that it was all so simple then
Or has time rewritten every line…
Memories may be beautiful and yet
What's too painful to remember
We simply choose to forget
                              –Hamlisch

These lyrics are ever-present in my head as guidance. I want to be vigilant not to overreach in my recollection of a time gone by. I want to get the story recounted just right—not too cold, not too hot. Perhaps the wisdom lies in that balance. When I view events in the balance, I am reminded that things were never as good or as bad as I may feel in the emotion of my recall. In many instances, the makeup of our memory has us recalling events as either more splendid or more disastrous than they really were. I try to keep in mind that just as my present-day life is a mix of good and bad, so too was my life in a time gone by. This perspective has been helpful in allowing me to celebrate my victories, as well as forgiving myself for losses and mistakes that were made in the past, and those yet to come.

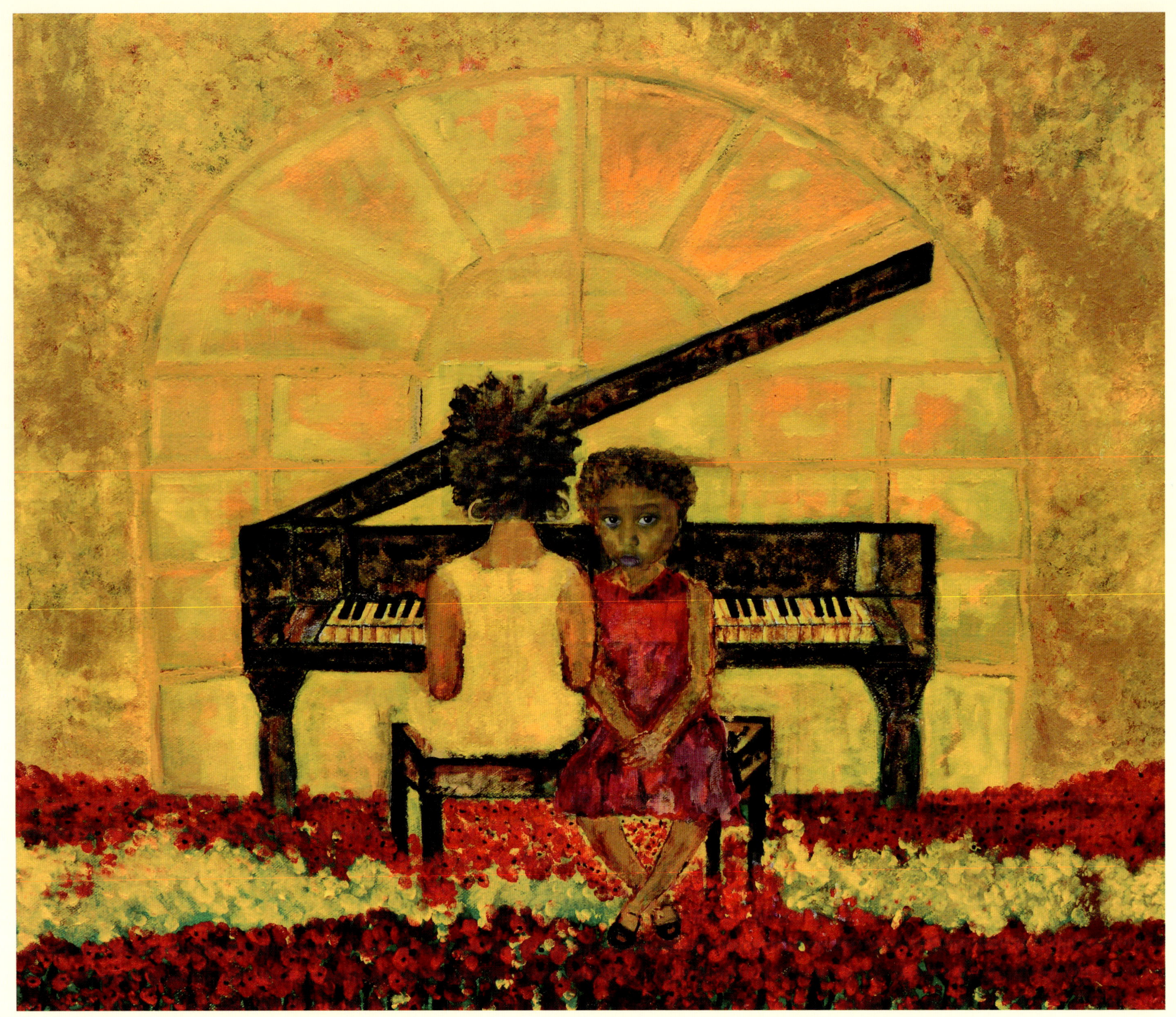

RECITAL

Acrylic and mixed materials on board
48" x 48"

THE FUTURE IS FORWARD

"You may give them your love, but not your thoughts.
For they have their own thoughts."

–Gibran

Kahlil Gibran offered that our children come through us, but they are not ours. Many times, those adorable creatures that we formerly knew do not resemble themselves as they grow up. Theirs is a world that my generation will never know, just as it was for the generation before us. Now, I barely recognize the young people in my life from when I was teaching them how to do this, that, and the other thing. Back then, I probably thought and hoped that we were building a monument to our interdependent relationship. I was not prepared for the day when our monument would fade into what sometimes feels like the irrelevancy of a long-abandoned statue in the park. I know that they must grow up, as I did. Perhaps their departure represents the necessary preparation for our children as they enter the world to come. Each generation is destined to struggle with this conflict that lies in letting go. We must accept that lessons to them in independence and self-direction, for better or worse, will one day include being independent from us as well.

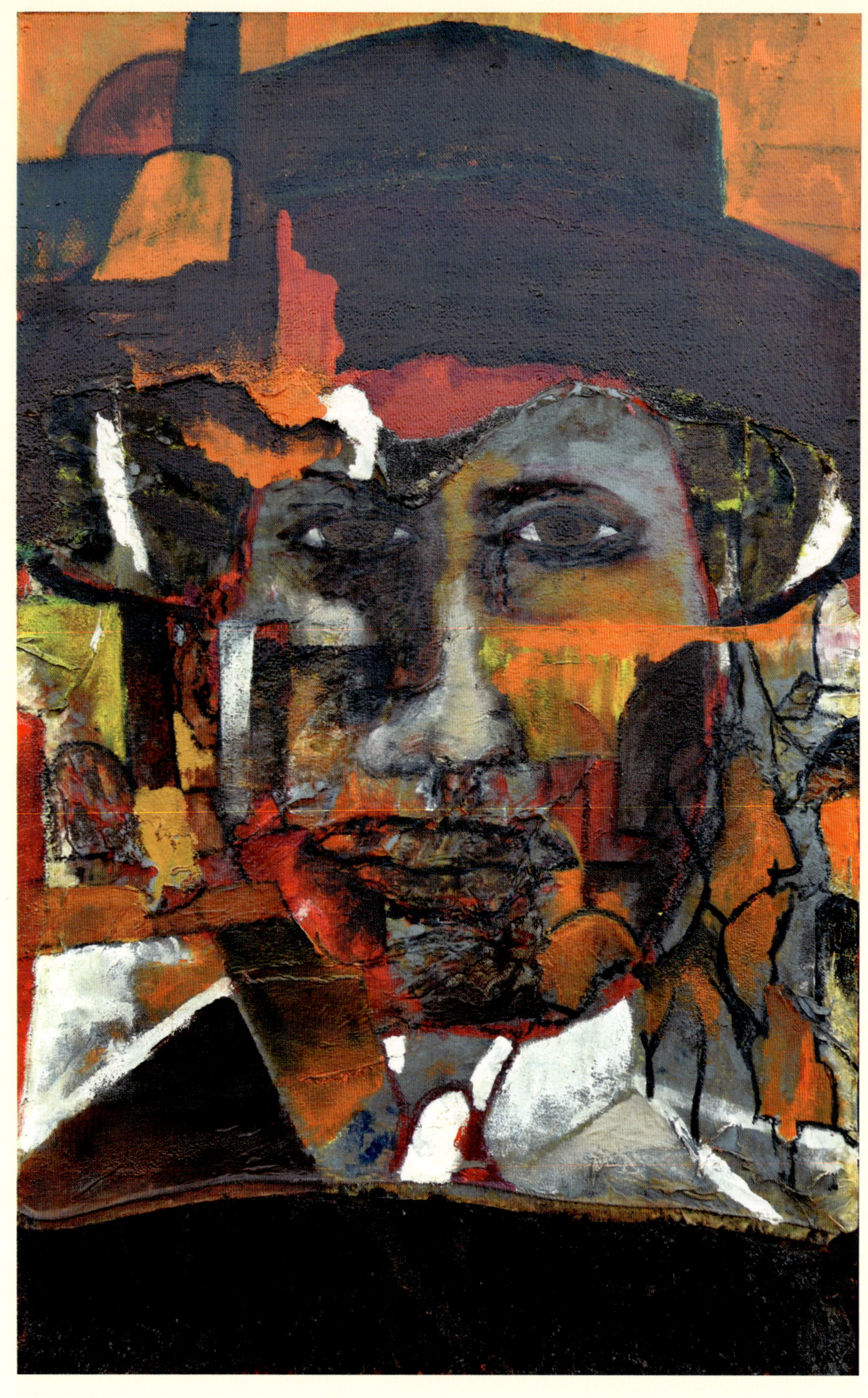

BOW

Acrylic and mixed materials on board
32" x 48"

SIMPLE PLEASURE

I have always loved food. My days are punctuated by breakfast, lunch, and dinner. The words "I forgot to eat" have never passed my lips. My portions are reasonable yet very consistent. Portion control and exercise empower me to get right back to my next feast.

I enjoy the ceremony of mealtime, starting with a cocktail, then perfectly pairing the food with wine, followed by a rich dessert and coffee, and perhaps closing it all out with my favorite cigar and bourbon, or rich liqueur if I am feeling a certain kinda way.

I am told that I am not truly a foodie because they have much higher discernment than I have. There are lines that foodies will not cross and places they will not eat, while I am discriminate only when I have choices. When I do not have a choice and my ever-present, lustful food-jones comes down on me, a bacon cheeseburger from the drive-through is in my near future. Most times, however, I decide to have a predictable meal at home instead of trying my luck out in the world of unknown outcomes.

During my workday, there are times that I retreat to the kitchen while I wait for the stock market to settle down if I am working as an investor, or for paint to dry if I am in the middle of a composition, or sometimes, I may just want something good to eat.

Not only do I adore most things food, I find myself at times evangelizing to others the joy of food as I experience it. I get full of the spirit and want to share my appetite and satisfaction. Family and friends visiting my home are always greeted with a drink and food. It is counterintuitive for me not to offer them something. Even when a meal is not present, the promise of one looms a few simple ingredients and the heat of my stovetop away.

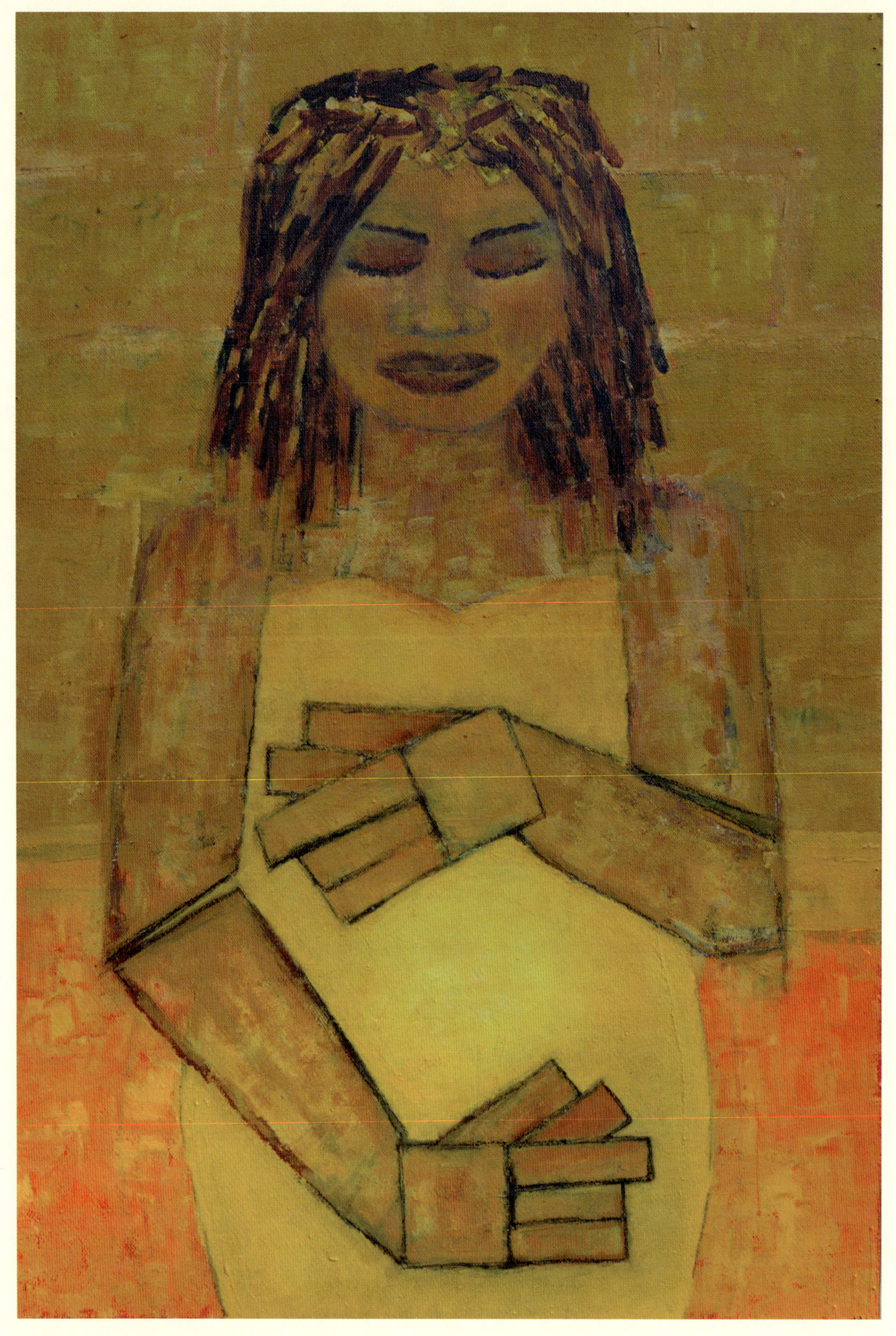

GLOW

Acrylic on board
32" x 48"

A SALUTE

I am the child of a single-parent household. There is data and ample commentary on the often-referred-to crisis of the so-called single-parent family. In some places, the term single parent is spoken as though it is a disability. Some commentary goes so far as to insist that having a two-parent household is the solution to everything that ails society, without regard to the quality of the recommended two parents. I am certain that there are some practical benefits to having two adults contributing financially to a household, as well as benefits gained by having another pair of mature eyes managing juvenile mischief. Being a single parent can be hard, and in an ideal world, having a partner for the family journey would be preferred. However, we should not lose sight of the victories and success stories of single mothers and fathers the world over. What is the wisdom of depreciating the good that *does* exist in favor of the perfect that is nonexistent or rare? The results that we are seeking may be driven more by the values that are promoted and enforced in a household instead of by a specific family composition.

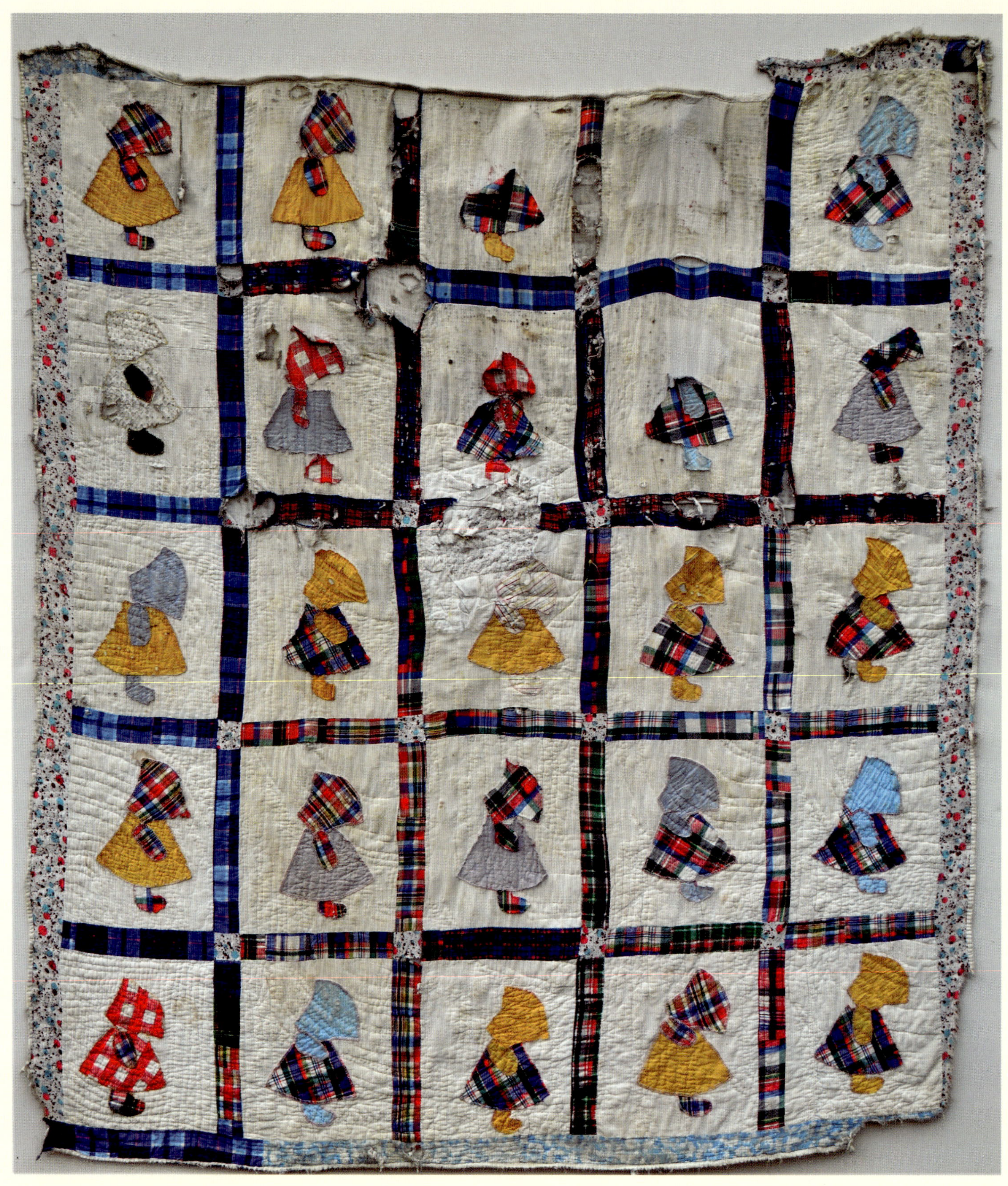

QUILT

70" x 80"

A METAPHOR

I inherited my first quilt from my father. It had Dutch maidens all in neat rows, five down and five across. I like quilts as a metaphor for our lives. With a quilt, you are connecting existing pieces to create a whole new thing. In our lives, we don't really get to start over. Succeed or fail, we are obliged to pick up where we are, try to salvage the best of our experiences, and move forward to begin again, and again, and then again.

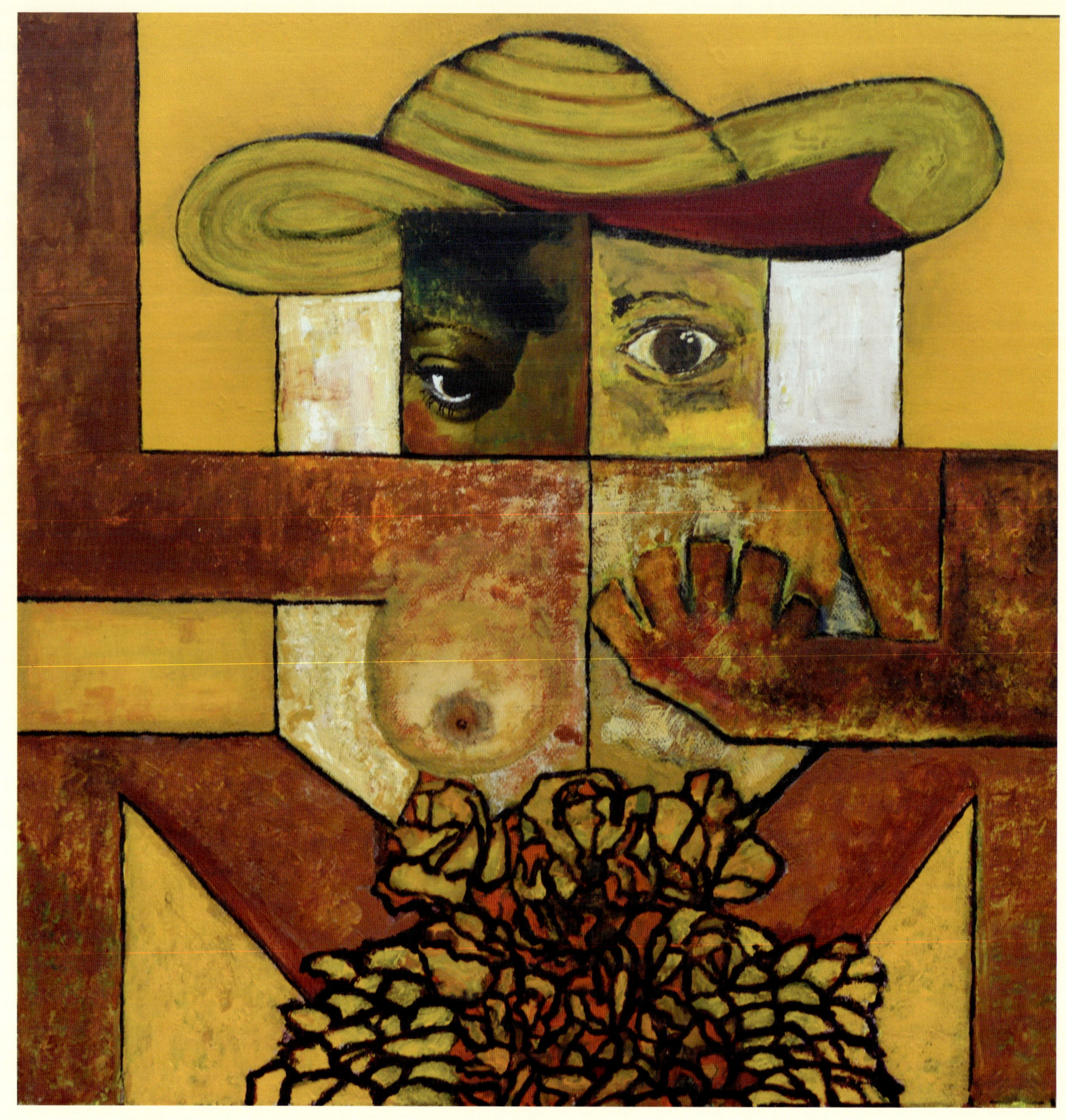

MIX

Acrylic and mixed materials on board
48" x 48"

A WHOLE PERSON

Each of us is a mixed bag of stuff. What might appear to be a bundle of contradictions at first glance is actually what makes us into a whole person. Our best parts are connected to another part that is at times difficult for others to accept. I try to hold that in mind in my relationships with others, as well as allowing a gentle space while in consideration of my whole self. Those viewed as steady and reliable often are also considered difficult and at times stern and cold. Then there are those who are charming and delightful but are often unpredictable and at times unreliable.

It is impossible for humans to be perfect in every way; we just aren't built that way. Our whole-person composition is what makes us into who and what we fully are. In the grand scheme, our parts may actually be more complementary than contradictory. Trying to have the very best part of what the next person offers, without the other stuff, may be as unlikely as when I want the perfection of pecan pie without the butterfat and calories. When you pick up one end of the stick, the other end follows.

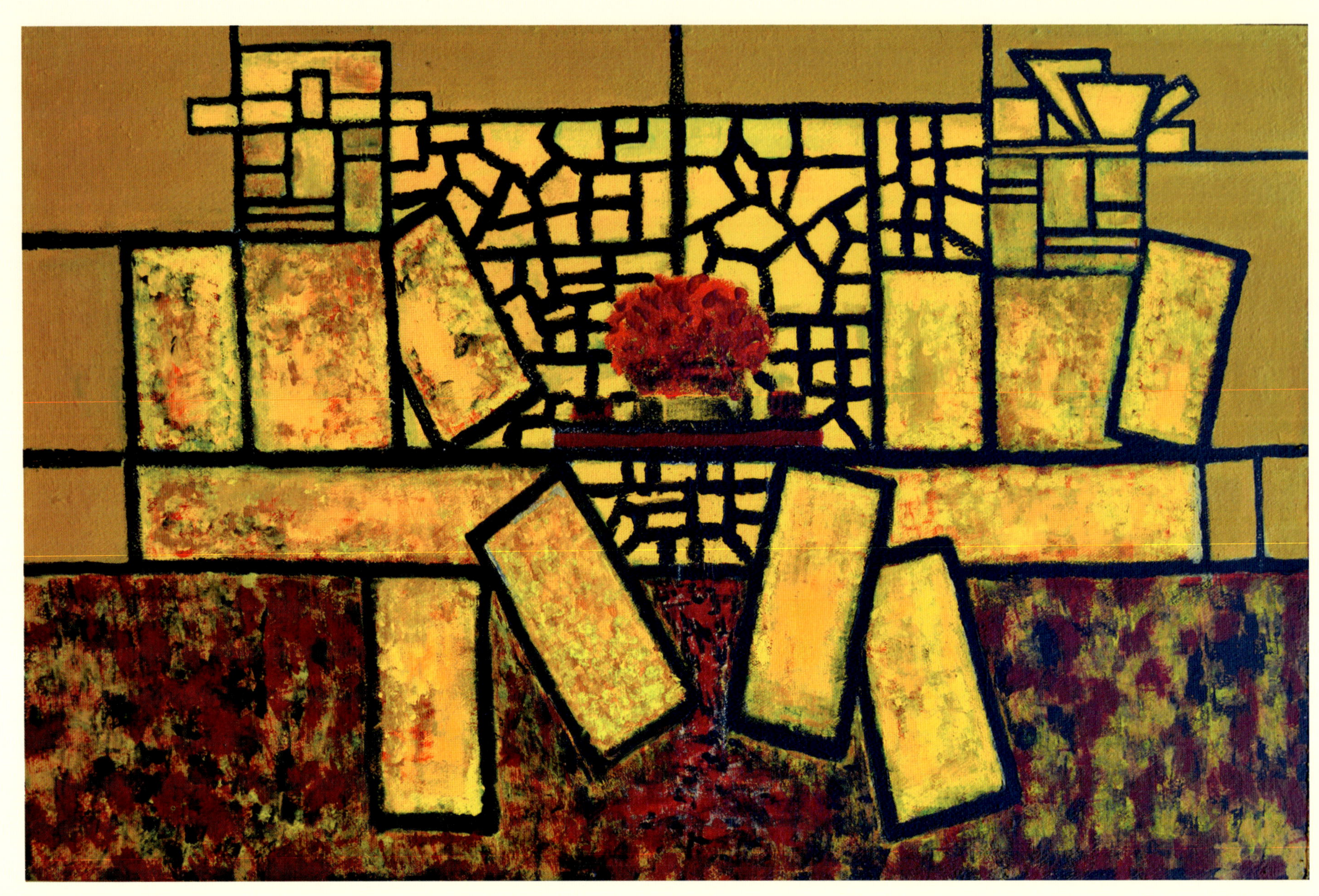

TEA

Acrylic on board
48" x 32"

GOSSIP

Gossip is idle talk or rumor, especially about the personal or private affairs of others; the act is also known as dishing, tattling, or, more recently, "spilling tea." Every day, there is as much good news in the world as bad news. It seems that bad news travels faster, because it is irresistible, for some, not only to receive but to distribute.

Recognizing the fundamental messiness and destructiveness of participating in gossip takes some of the fun out of it… but not all of it, and just incrementally so. We all enjoy gossip to varying degrees. Some of us search for it, some create it, and then there are those who wait for it to come to them. I get it; we are all drawn to scandal and spectacle, myself included. I don't go looking for gossip, but if some shows up, I will pull up a chair and listen. Especially after I sanction the exchange with a "bless his heart," or "I really feel bad for him." For a long time, I felt that most gossip was just a "fun" distraction from the monotony or despair of our own lives. I have, however, become a bit troubled by the potential harm it can wreak in our village. Participating in trash-passing depreciates all of us. When gossip is delivered to me, I wonder just what it is about me that has motivated the person to offer this untidiness. I also consider that the person who trades in scandal with me will do the same against me in other places.

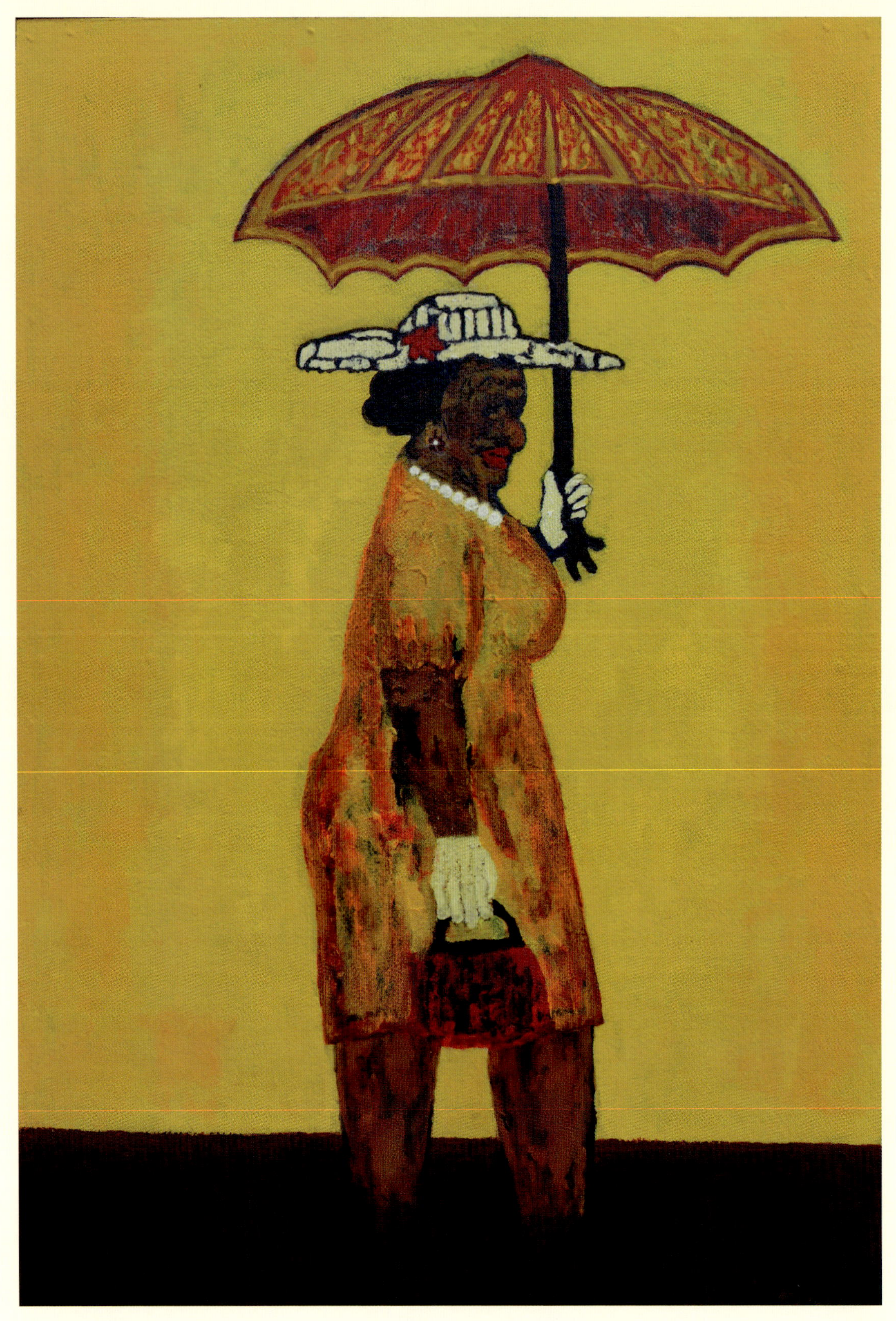

MS. VI

Acrylic on board
32" x 48"

MS. VIOLET BENNETT

Ms. Vi always maintained a regal bearing in 1960s Pine Bluff, Arkansas. I loved to see her coming and hated to see her leave. She appeared properly at arm's length with most everyone in her tone and manner, except me. One of my favorite parts of our relationship was that I appeared to have all of who she was to myself. She always had time and space for her "Sunny Boy." I never knew her to have any family locally. Although she would on rare occasion speak of having family in some distant place, I never met them. As far as I was concerned, I was her family.

In memory of Ms. Violet Bennett (1902–1975)

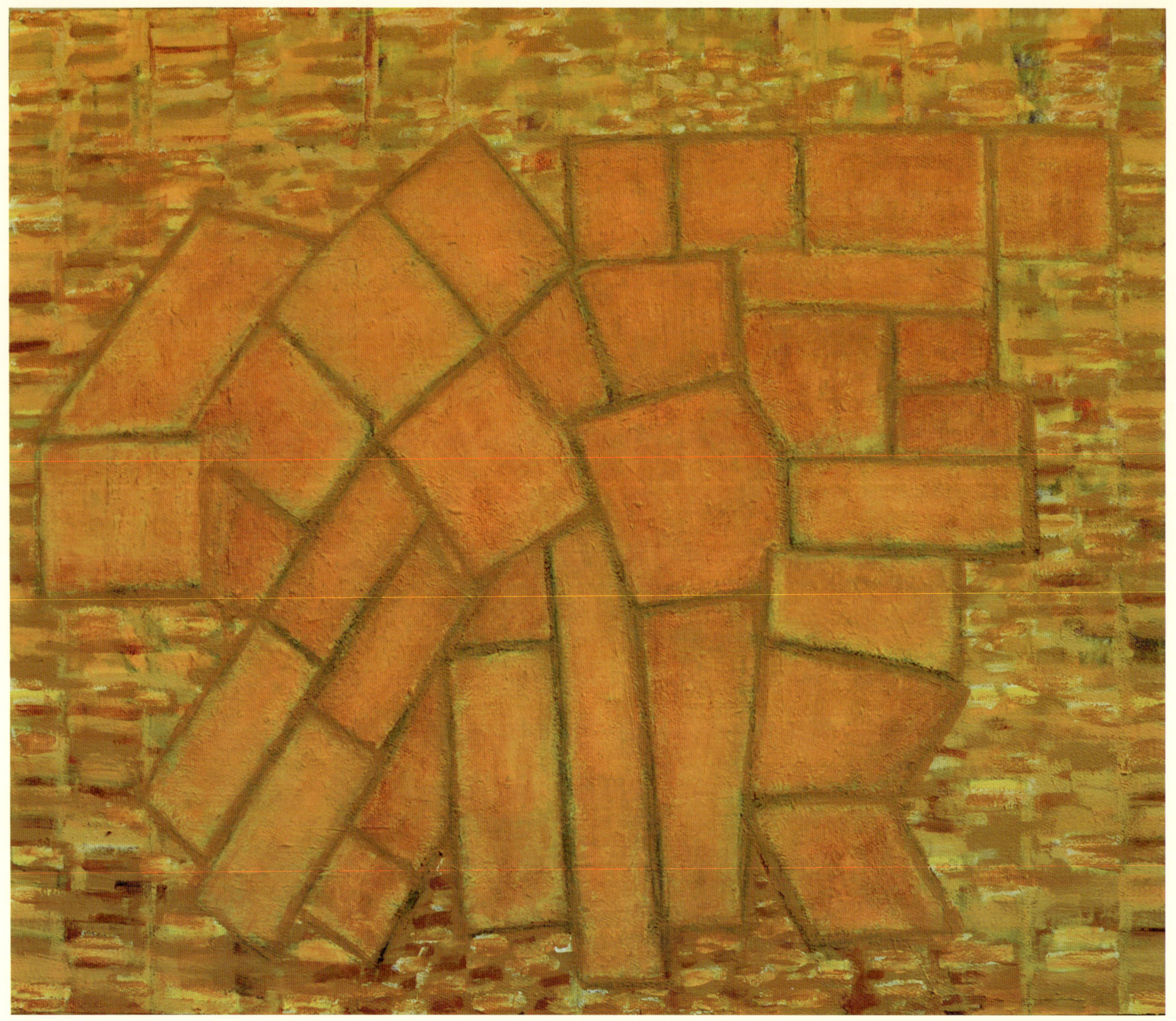

TRIBE

Acrylic on board
48" x 48"

MERGING OF EQUALS

I am the tenth of the thirteen children my mother delivered to this world. It is amazing how different each of us is in so many ways. We all grew up eating the same food, being taught the same values, and receiving the same discipline, yet we are so different from each other. There appears to be one of us for each category of humanity. This reality is difficult to accept with my family members, because I want us to be in the same choir, the same robe, and singing from the same hymnal. But that ain't necessarily so.

Fortunately for any of us, whether it is a family member or a neighbor down the street, most differences are not necessarily good or bad, right or wrong, black or white; they may just be different.

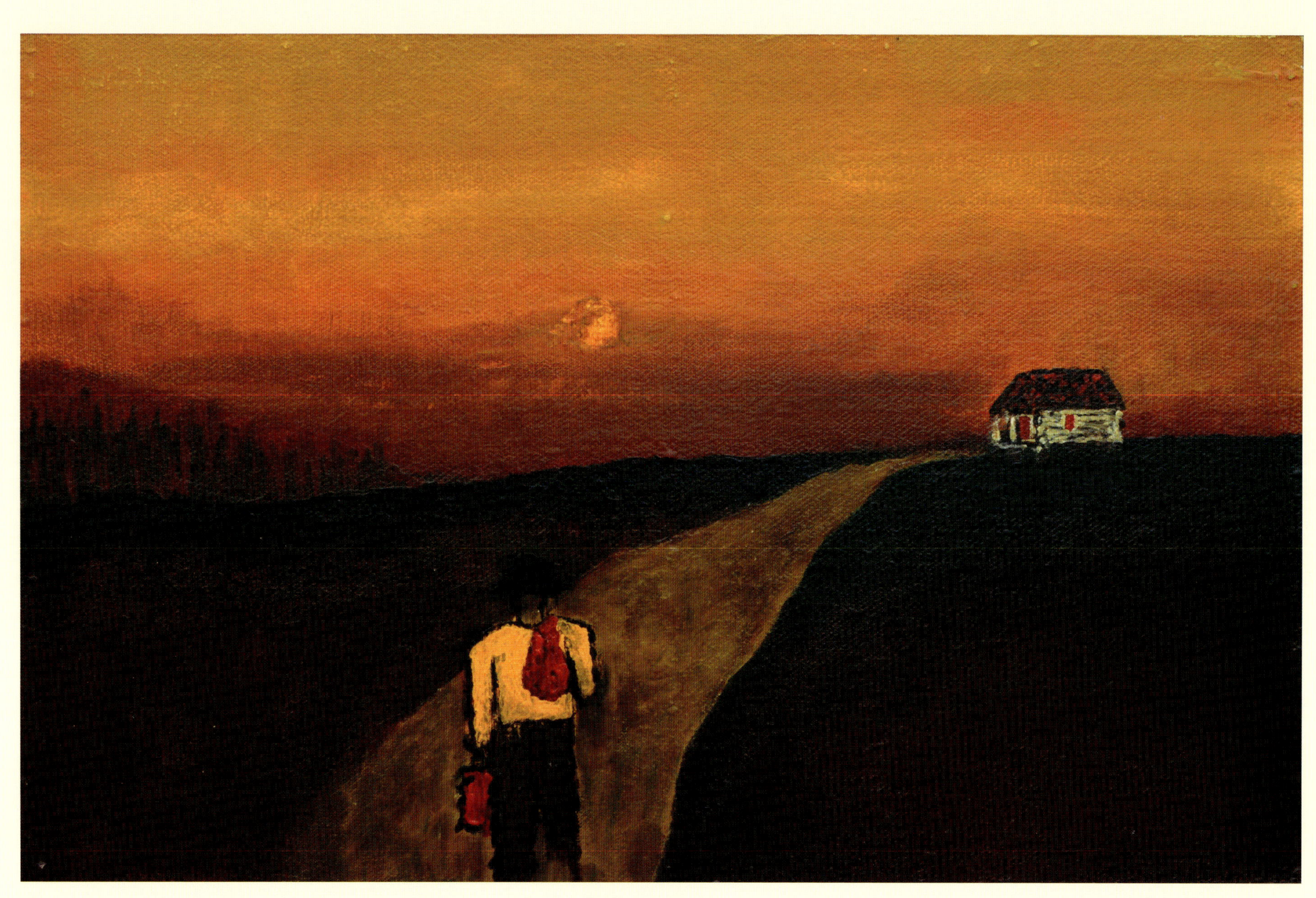

MAN

Acrylic on board
48" x 32"

I came here because this is the only place I know...

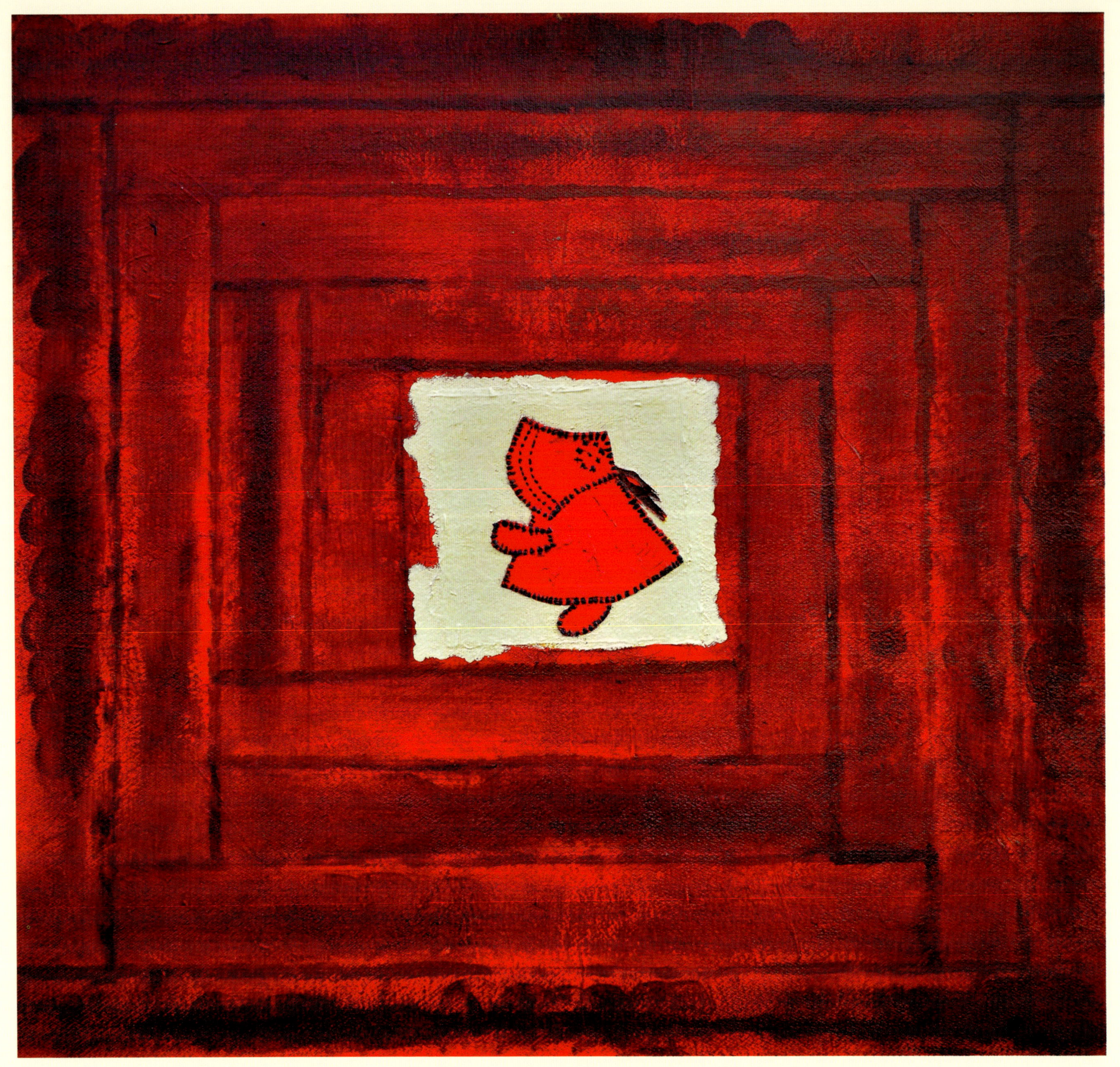

RED MAIDEN

Acrylic and mixed materials on board
48" x 48"

SIMPLE SAUCE

My recipes are not complicated and rarely require much time to prepare. Within an hour after I enter my kitchen, "I needs to be feeling satisfaction." I prefer to spend time with my meal companions rather than wearing myself out preparing the meal. And then there are other times when I just want to eat without too much delay. I would drag it out if I thought time and elaborate preparation added to my satisfaction, but they do not.

A traditional Bolognese Sauce is usually a simple red sauce with meat added, until it enters a Southern man's kitchen. Then, this is what happens:

Two Pounds Browned and Chopped Ground Sausage	Tablespoon Onion Powder
Large Chopped Bell Pepper	Tablespoon Garlic Powder
Large Chopped Whole Onion	Half-Cup Chopped Garlic
Tablespoon Oregano	Two Cups Tomato Sauce
Tablespoon Basil	Two Cups Chopped Tomatoes
Half-Tablespoon Black Pepper	Half-Cup Brown Sugar
Half-Tablespoon Red Pepper Flakes	Half-Cup Honey

Once I brown the sausage and drain the fat, I add the bell peppers, onions and spices, followed by the chopped garlic, tomato sauce, chopped tomatoes, brown sugar, and honey. This mixture should be cooked at medium-low heat until it reaches a boil. Reduce to low and allow it to simmer.

After about thirty minutes, remove from fire and allow the sauce to rest. Resting is the process of cooling down, an important step for most dishes, especially those containing meat, because it seems to allow the flavor and texture to settle into itself.

While waiting for the sauce to rest, I can prepare angel hair pasta, al dente. The spice and heat of the sauce plays well with a Malbec or Cabernet.

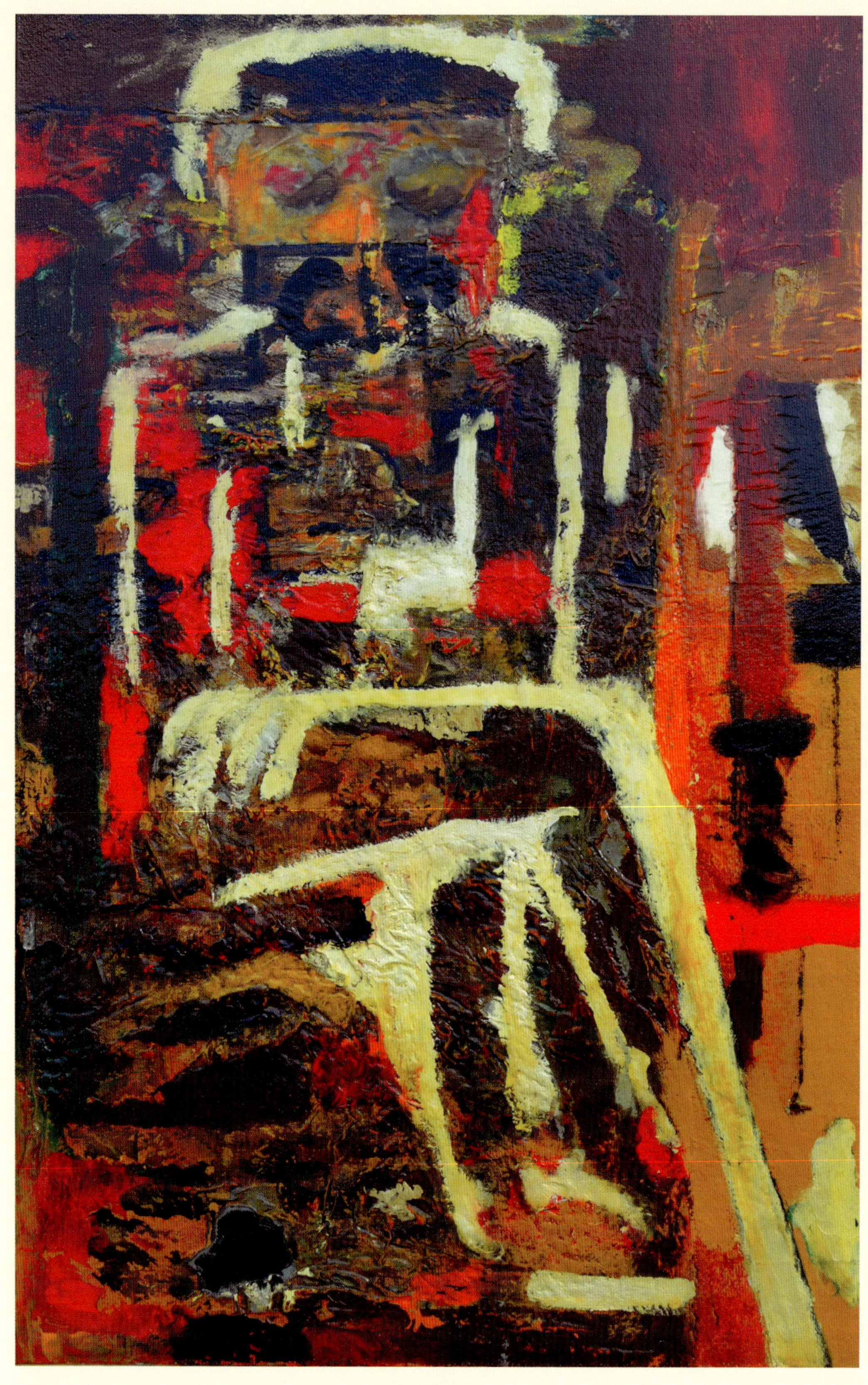

SMOKE

Acrylic and mixed materials on board
32" x 48"

No man is an island,
Entire of itself,
Every man is a piece of the continent,
A part of the main.

–Donne

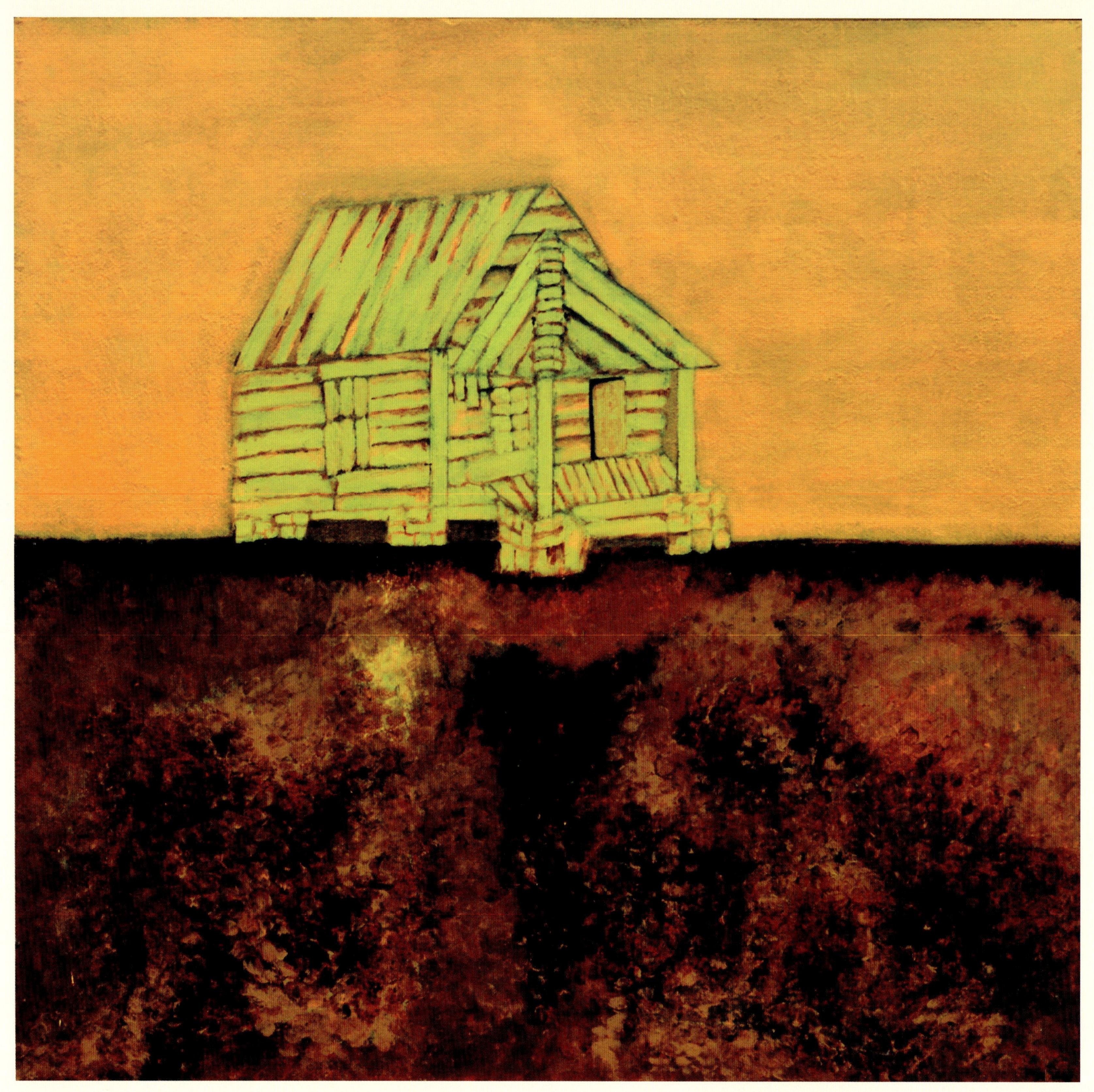

ONE-HALF

Acrylic and mixed materials on board
48" x 48"

A SPECIAL PLACE

When you walk down East Thirteenth Street like you are headed toward town, just past Curbow's Fish Market, over there near the washateria across from Norris Dean Jarmon's house, you will come upon 505 Thirteenth Street on the right side of the road. There is a path of beaten-down grass in the space that separates 505 and 503. At path's end, you will find a house numbered 505 and ½. This simple structure contained a small bed, a sink, a toilet, and a small stove. This was my father's home and the place I came to visit him as a young boy. It was dull and quiet in comparison to my mother's house, with none of the traffic and excitement of children everywhere, but it held many of my most vibrant childhood memories. This was where I learned that you really should wait for adult supervision for fireworks, because if you don't, you will receive a small burn on your forefinger that will leave a blemish for life. I learned that weenies (hot dogs) really do need to be roasted, because if you sneak and eat them cold, you will be awake throughout the night throwing up. It is also where I discovered that if you watch the radio long enough, after a while, all the characters will appear within the space that you are in.

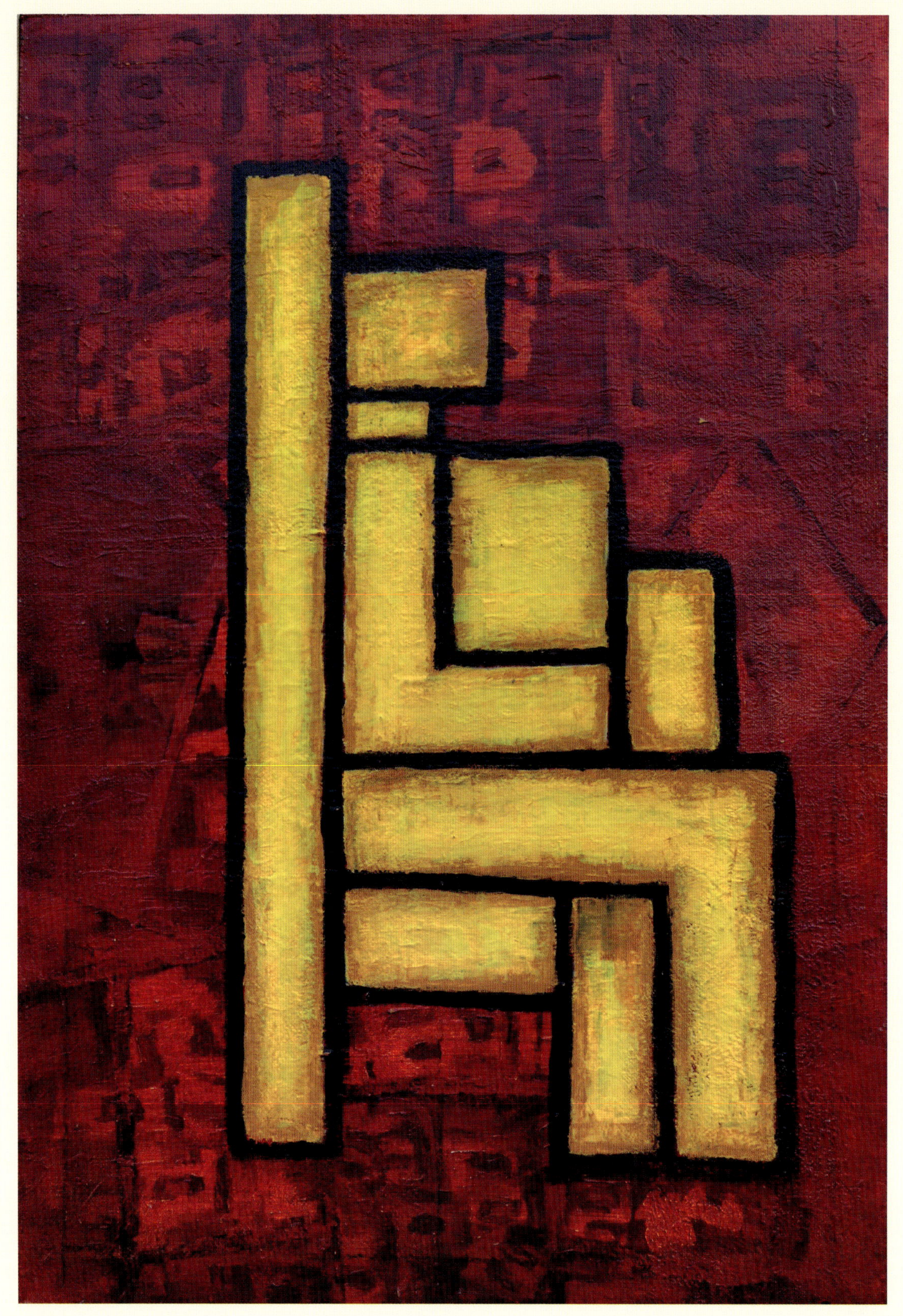

SOLO

Acrylic on board
32" x 48"

SELF-RELIANCE

Early on, I sought others to help, guide, and fix me, with very little success. It appears that those who could help me did not, and those who wanted to help me could not. I try not to lose sight of the very real probability that most people can hardly manage their own lives, let alone positively impact the lives of others. I discovered that I may be the one I am looking for to do all of this helping, guiding, and fixing. I have not fully foreclosed the notion that someone may one day be my hero just in time. Meanwhile, I am going to trust myself to do for myself.

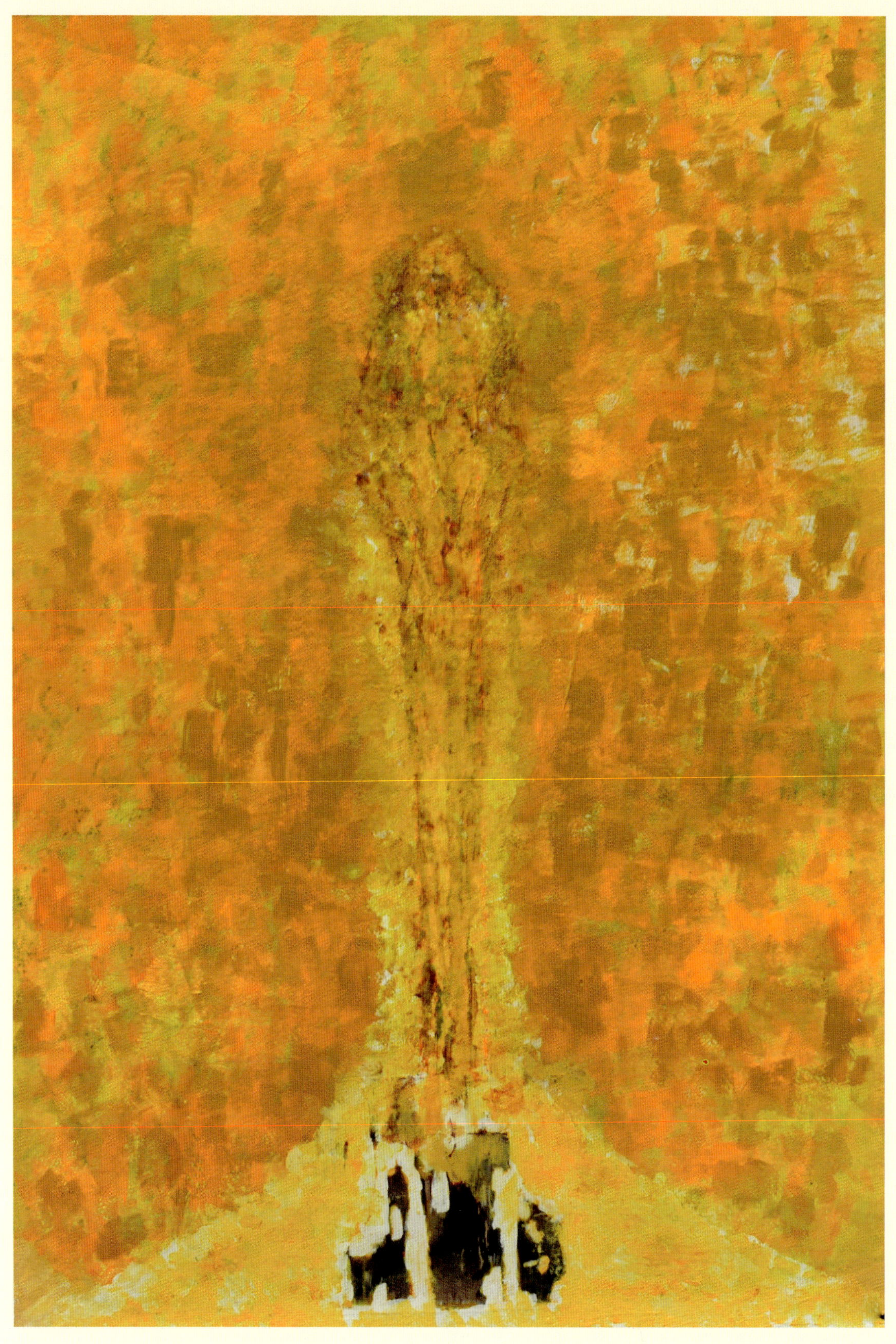

YELLAH

Acrylic and mixed materials on board
32" x 48"

Love is not love
Which alters when it alteration finds,
Or bends with the remover to remove…
                                    –Shakespeare

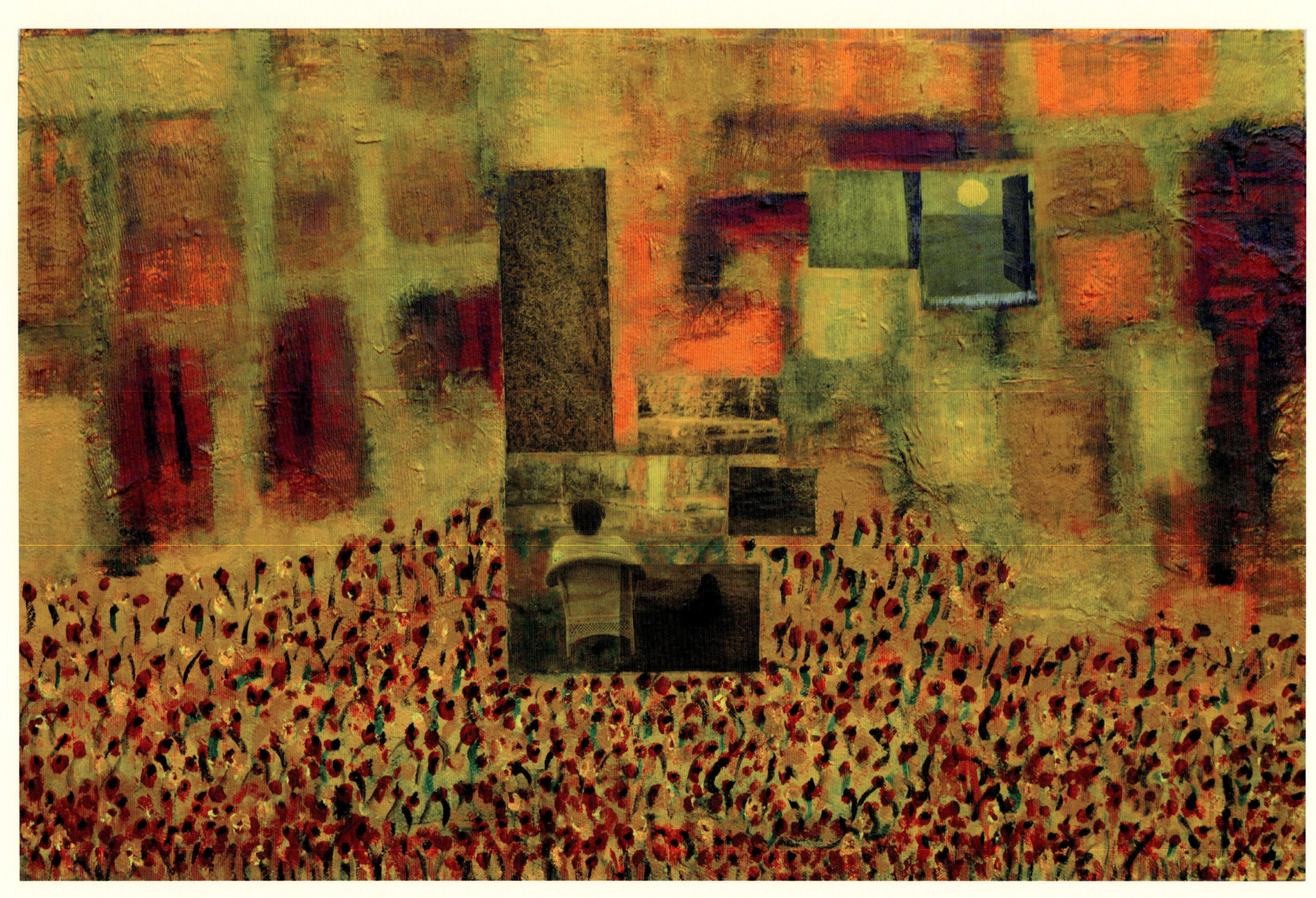

SUE

Acrylic and mixed materials on board
48" x 32"

SUE

Every dog owner says they have the best dog ever, and I am sure that we are all correct. Even if our dog is full of imperfections, we remain charmed and fascinated by this creature that has entered our life. When I first met her at the animal shelter, she jumped into my lap with a toy and stared at me with an "I'm the one you're looking for, let's get out of here" look, and we did.

For twelve years, Sue and I lived a fun-filled and eventful life. Always one thing and then another in the never-dull culture of a dog and her human. In later years, there came a time that my dear Sue could no longer run fast or jump high (nor could I). These diminished abilities were not cause for either of us to abandon the other. Sue-girl remained my dear little puppy dog, no matter her age or condition.

I don't keep pictures of Sue on my phone or in my wallet to show off to unsuspecting people; however, I do use her as illustration in some of my writing and art workshops that I have with children. I share with them a chapter of my life, with my Sue as an exercise in storytelling.

As I was packing up following one of those workshops, I turned, and there stood this little person, knee-high to me, with dark hair and big eyes. She was holding the drawing and story of her own dog, angling it upward the length of my seven-foot frame for me to see. She said, "I had a puppy too, but he died. I really liked him a lot, but he died." I whispered my reply to her that my puppy had died also. I confided that I did not announce Sue's recent death when I read my story, because it makes me sad. Then, my new little friend said, "I know, huh."

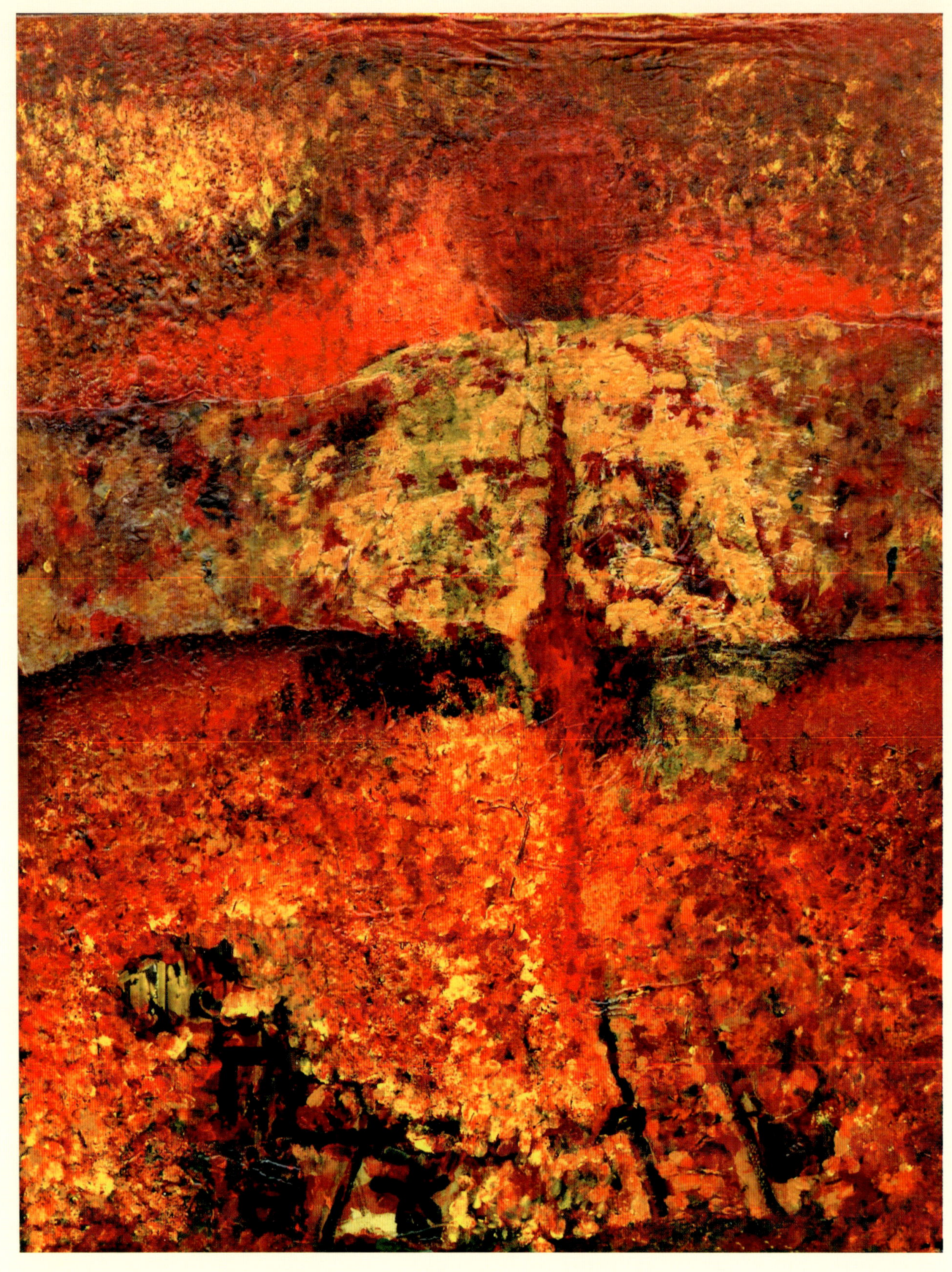

RED

Acrylic and mixed materials on board
38" x 48"

FIRE

As philosophical as any of us may be on a variety of topics, we only learn what we are made of when we go through the test of fire. We only discover our true character and composition when ideas move from rhetorical flourishes to the light of day and we are summoned to walk our talk.

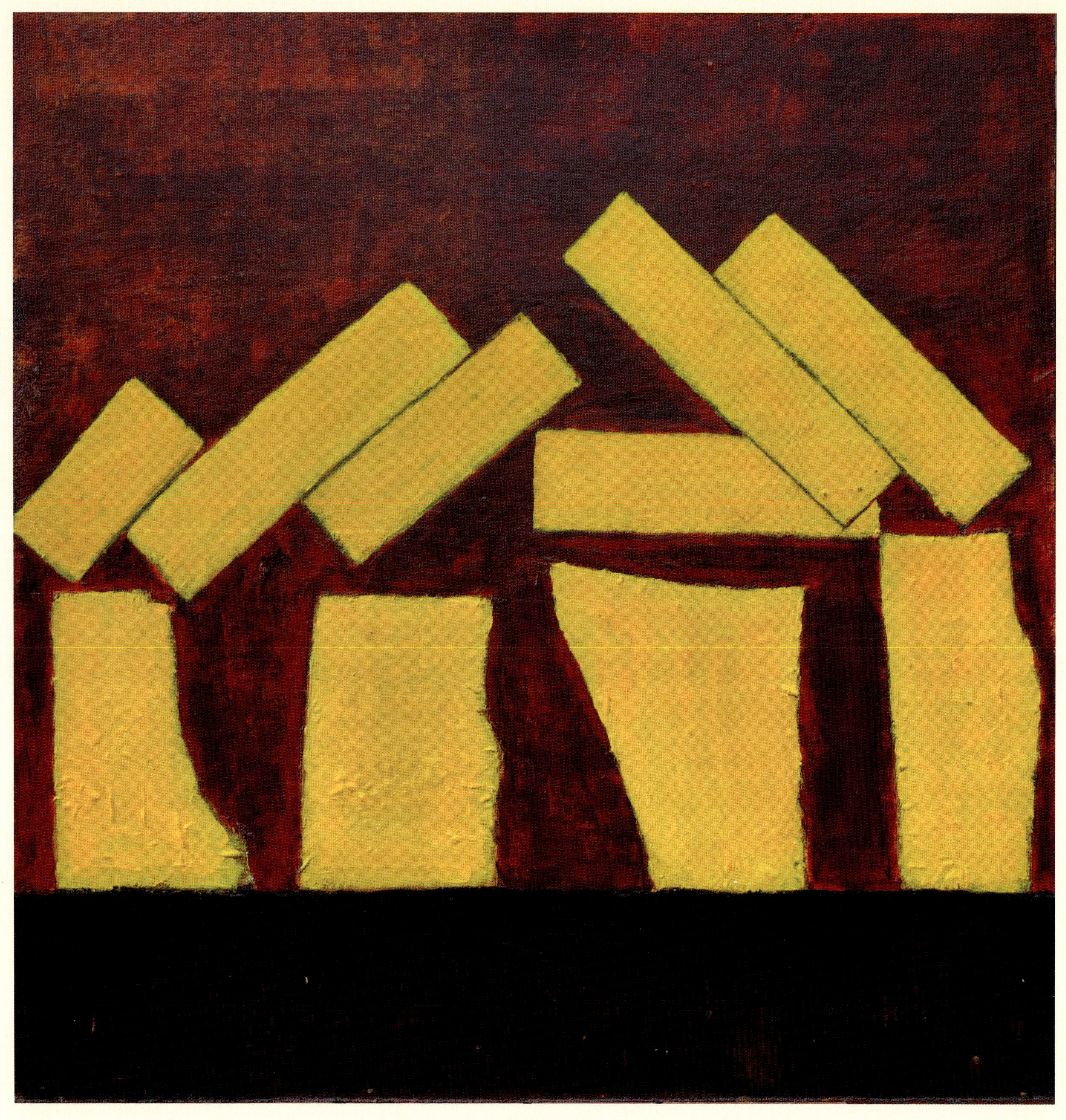

RUIN

Acrylic on board
48" x 48"

METES AND BOUNDS

Sometimes, it appears that people lust after money as though it is a tonic for all that ails them in life. Money can improve certain parts of the human condition, but a cash injection is different from making everything just right. If you need money for a particular thing, money can satisfy that, but it is not a solution to unhappiness or discontent. Furthermore, after you sit for a while with your newfound station full of money, you may discover that instead of fixing everything, you are simply left with a new normal. Being rich will not necessarily improve you; it may only amplify the person you already are. If you are not kind, then having more money just makes you a rich, yet unkind person. If you are a kind person, then having more money can help you be kind in many more places and in grand ways.

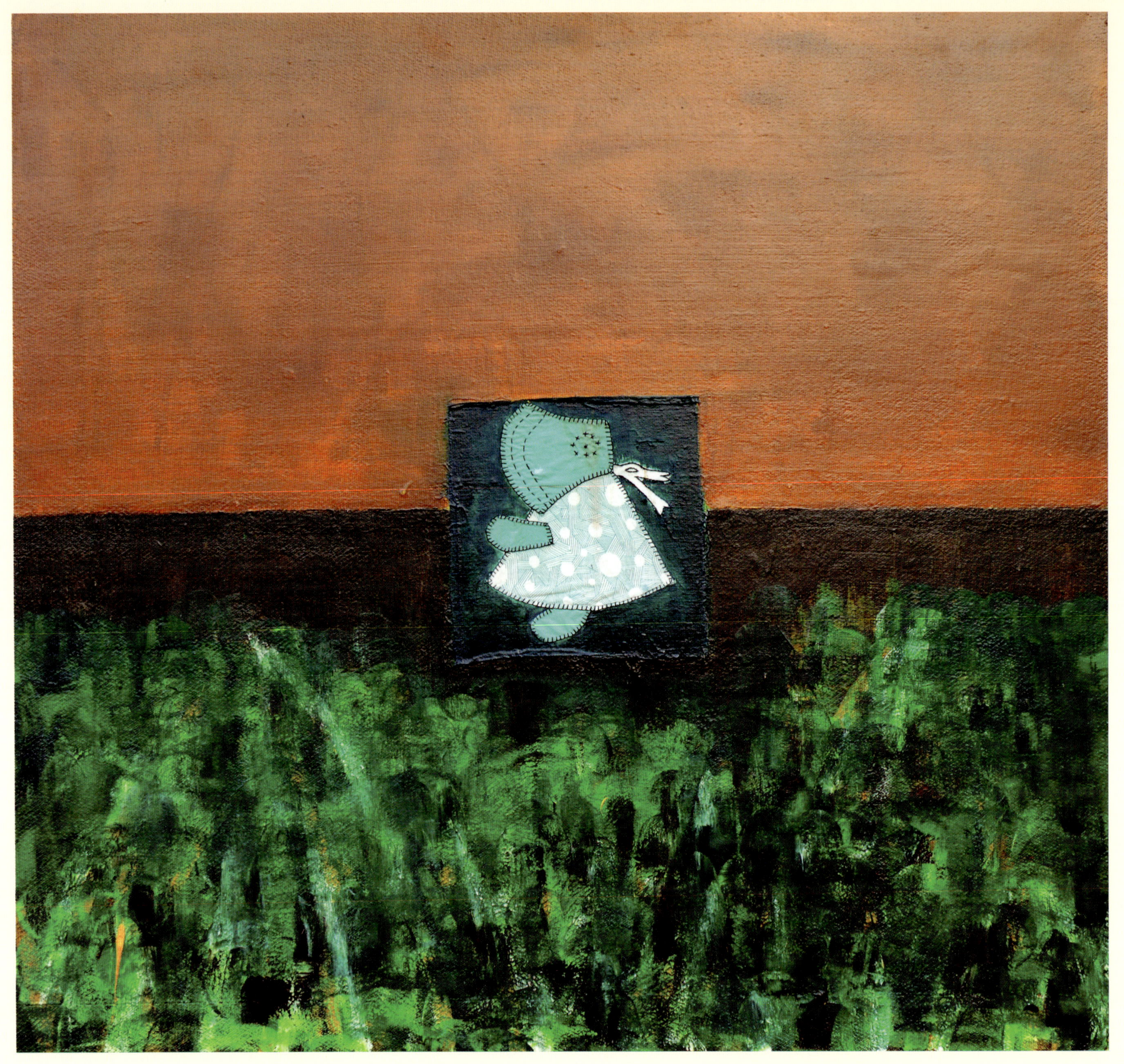

GREEN MAIDEN

Acrylic and mixed materials on board
48" x 48"

COLLARDS

This is not your Big Mama's recipe. Many southerners grew up discovering a huge chunk of glistening fatback swimming in melted collard greens greeting them when they removed the cover from the pot on the stovetop. When I was a child, I was grateful for supper, however it came to me. Now, not so much. My version of collards does not include fatback or any other protein; ample taste and seasoning will be derived from the spices. Nor do the greens require all day to cook.

One Bunch Collard Greens, stems removed, washed and shredded

Whole Chopped Onion

Cup Minced Garlic

Half-Cup Olive Oil

Two Cups Chopped Tomatoes

Third-Cup Onion Powder

Third-Cup Garlic Powder

Two Tablespoons Black Pepper

Half-Tablespoon Red Pepper Flakes

Half-Cup Brown Sugar

Four Cups Water

Two Tablespoons Vegetable Bouillon

Layer all the ingredients in your favorite large pot, then cover. Cook at medium-low for an hour. Then, simmer for half an hour or to your desired tenderness.

Collard greens are probably incomplete without the texture of hot-water cornbread:

Cup Cornmeal

Level Teaspoon Baking Powder

Half-Cup Chopped Walnuts

Half-Cup Cranberries

Cup Hot Water

Egg, beaten

Tablespoon Olive Oil

Combine cornmeal, baking powder, walnuts and cranberries. Add hot water to dry mixture, and blend well. Add beaten egg and olive oil. Use additional oil to cover the surface of a skillet. Cook evenly on each side as you would a pancake. Mmmm!

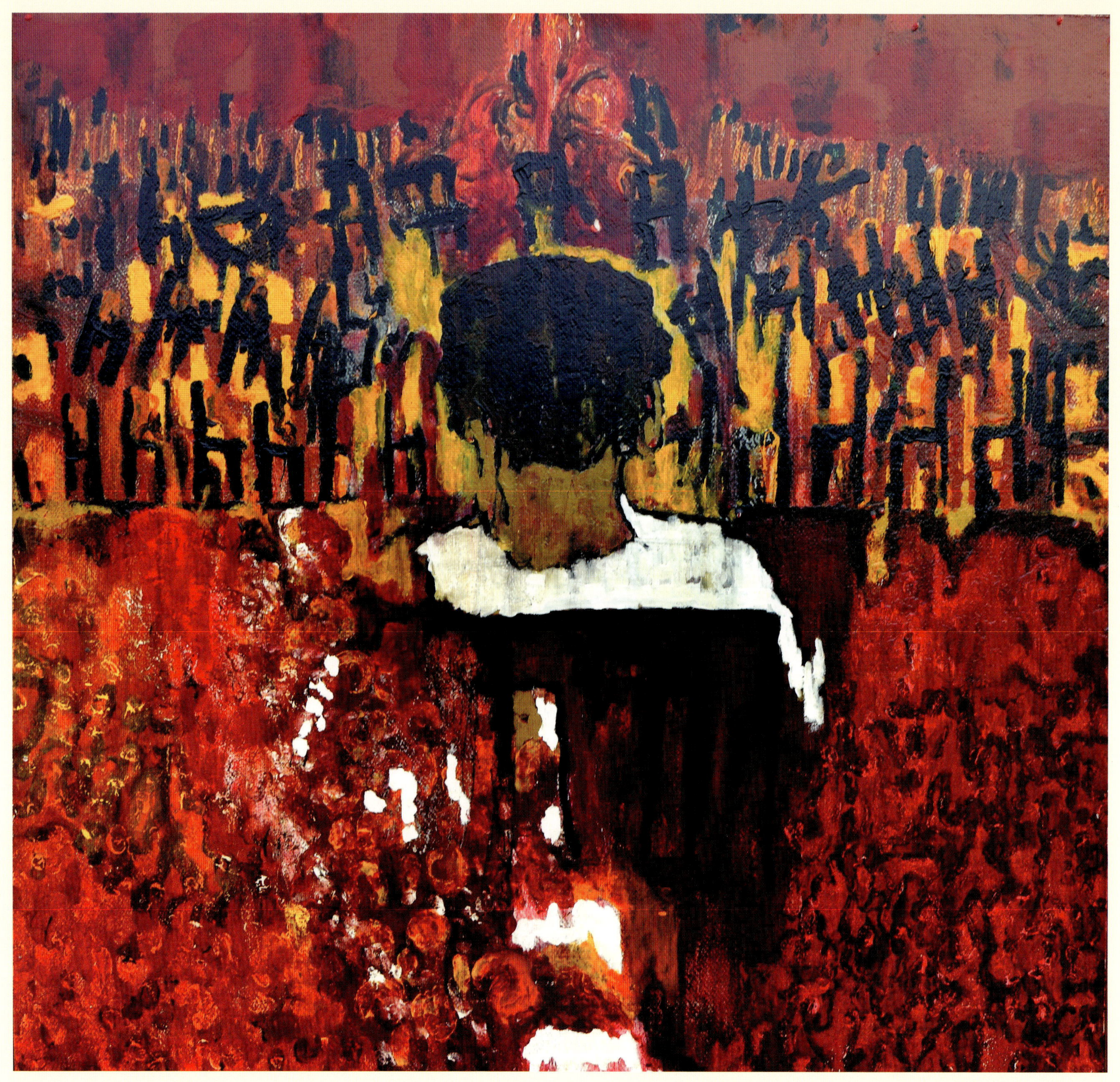

LA SCALA

Acrylic on board
48" x 48"

TICK TOCK

—Raitt

The elders have counseled over the years, "You just keep on living; there will come a day that will bring with it change." Right they were.

I discover myself in a certain place along with my contemporaries. For as enlightened as my perspective is about this change of season that I find myself in as I age, it leaves me a little, if not a lot, sad.

We were all so beautiful and able in a time gone by, in our spirit if not our reality. Now, our stride is less sturdy than it once was. What was once our warm-up has evolved into our main event. Our run may have morphed into a jog, only to become a walk, followed by the comfort of being seated in our favorite chair. The simple movement from one place to the other can at times require a concentrated calculation punctuated by grunts, groans, and deep breathing.

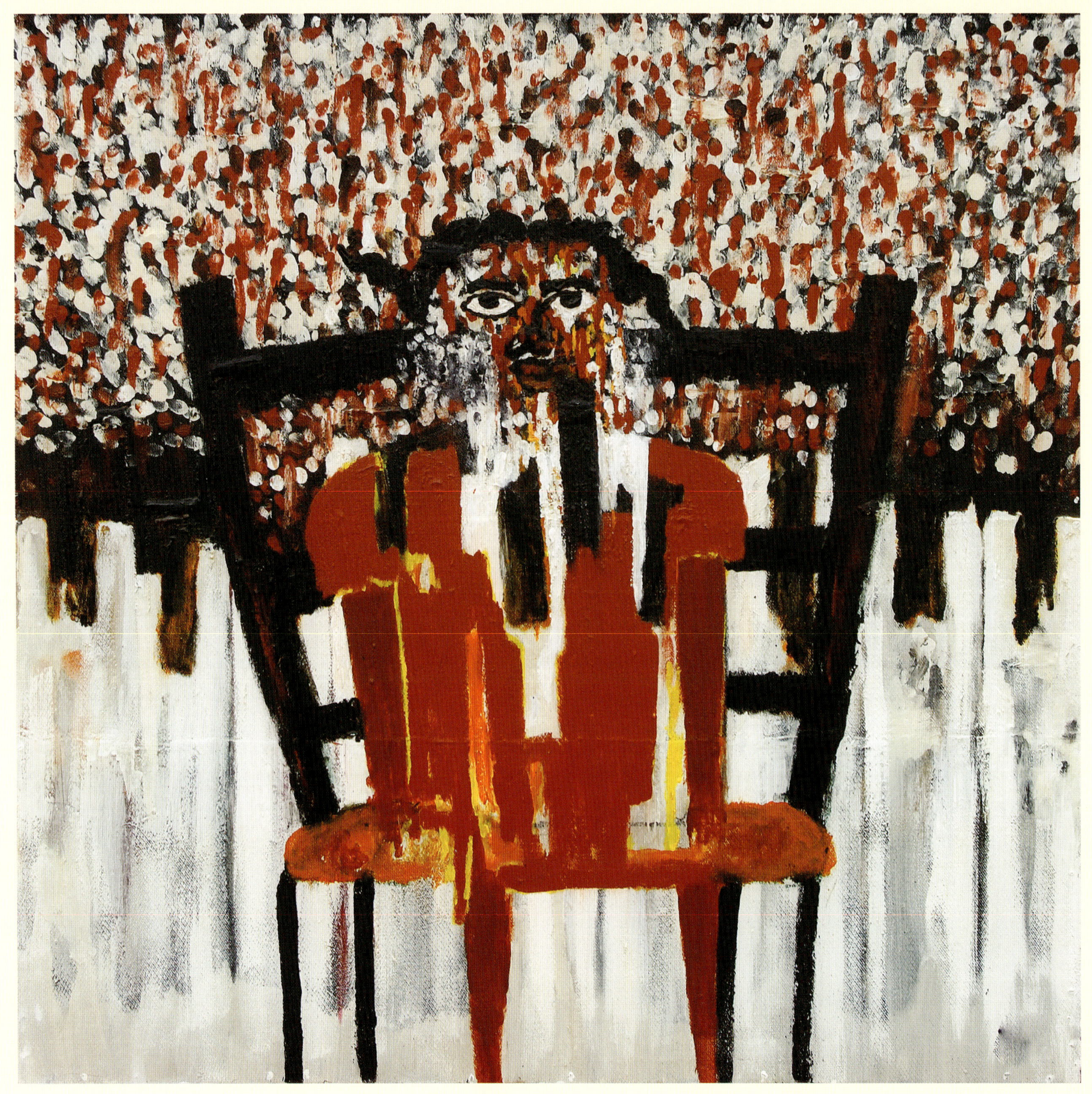

GIRL IN CHAIR

Acrylic on board
48" x 48"

TENDER CARE

There are many buses throughout the world delivering children home at the end of each school day. On the street where I live, I find myself looking for a particular bus. As I sit there in the halted traffic, I observe the ritual that I have witnessed many times before. The bus slows and then stops; red lights and paddles extend in front of my neighbor's home. No less than three family members from inside the house make their way to welcome the light of their collective life with the enthusiasm reserved for a conquering hero returning to the village. I am guessing that the star of this show of love and admiration is a special-needs child, if I am to judge by the shape of the bus and the accompanying reclined wheelchair. My heart is full as I witness this ritual of tender care and mercy. We all want this expression for ourselves; how lovely when we choose to share it with others. In a world that can be so cold and rough, I am encouraged that all is not lost.

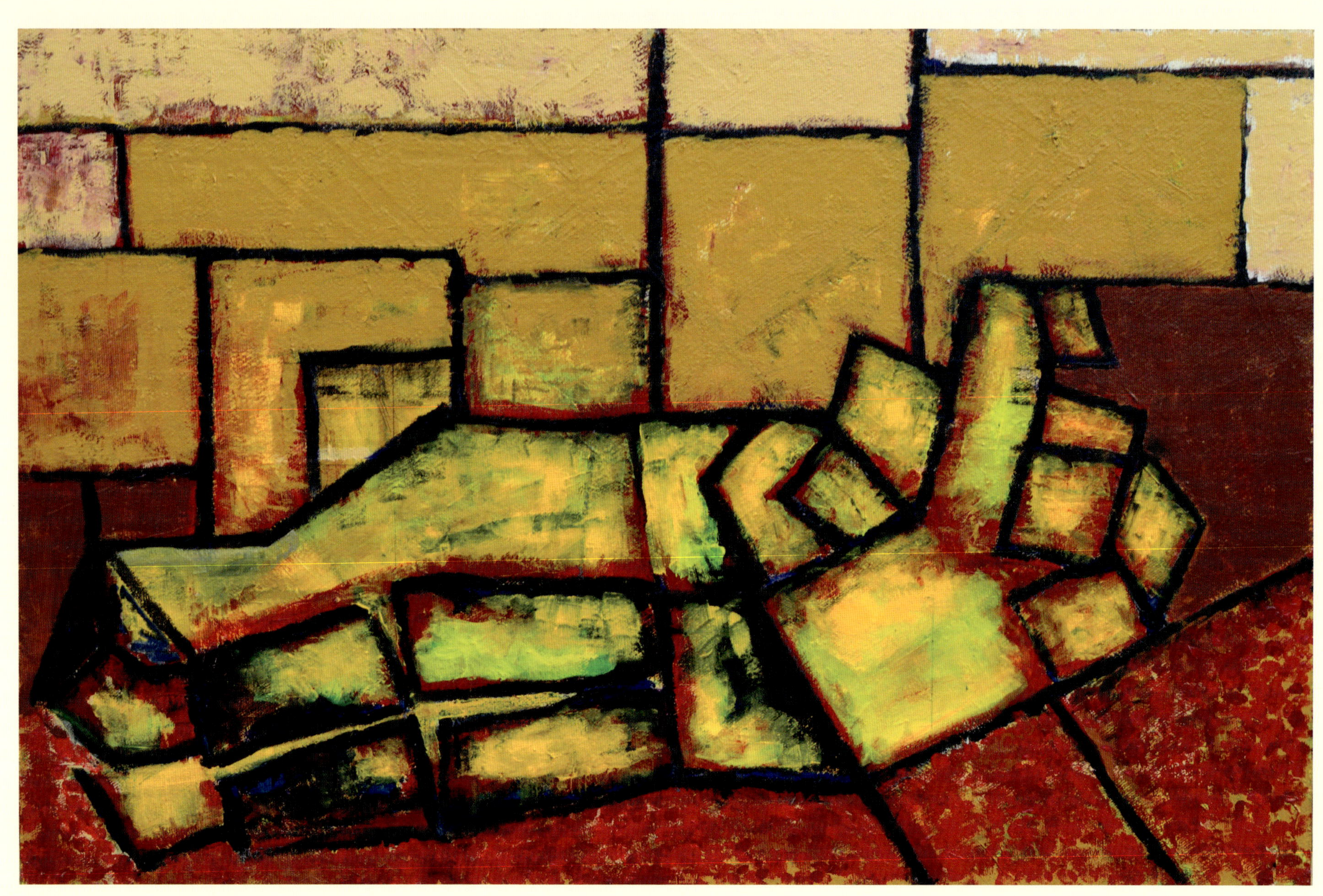

DUÉ

Acrylic on board
48" x 32"

EQUALING OF YOKE

I had spent the better part of an afternoon listening to a friend walk me through the frustrations she was having with her man. She closed out her narrative of woe to say that it would do her no good to leave him and the relationship they shared, because she would only spend the rest of her life looking for him or someone just like him. Her closing lament was, "I love him so…"

Our intimate relationships represent much of our life's consumption. Our desire for love and the promise of love is evergreen. While we may become frustrated with a particular relationship or even suspend our quest for the at-times-elusive mighty love, the desire remains.

If we are wise, we may conclude that no person is absolutely perfect, but there may be one perfect person for us. We should be hopeful that we see something in that person to keep us inspired through hell or high water, something proving this relationship is a fundamental necessity to our lives.

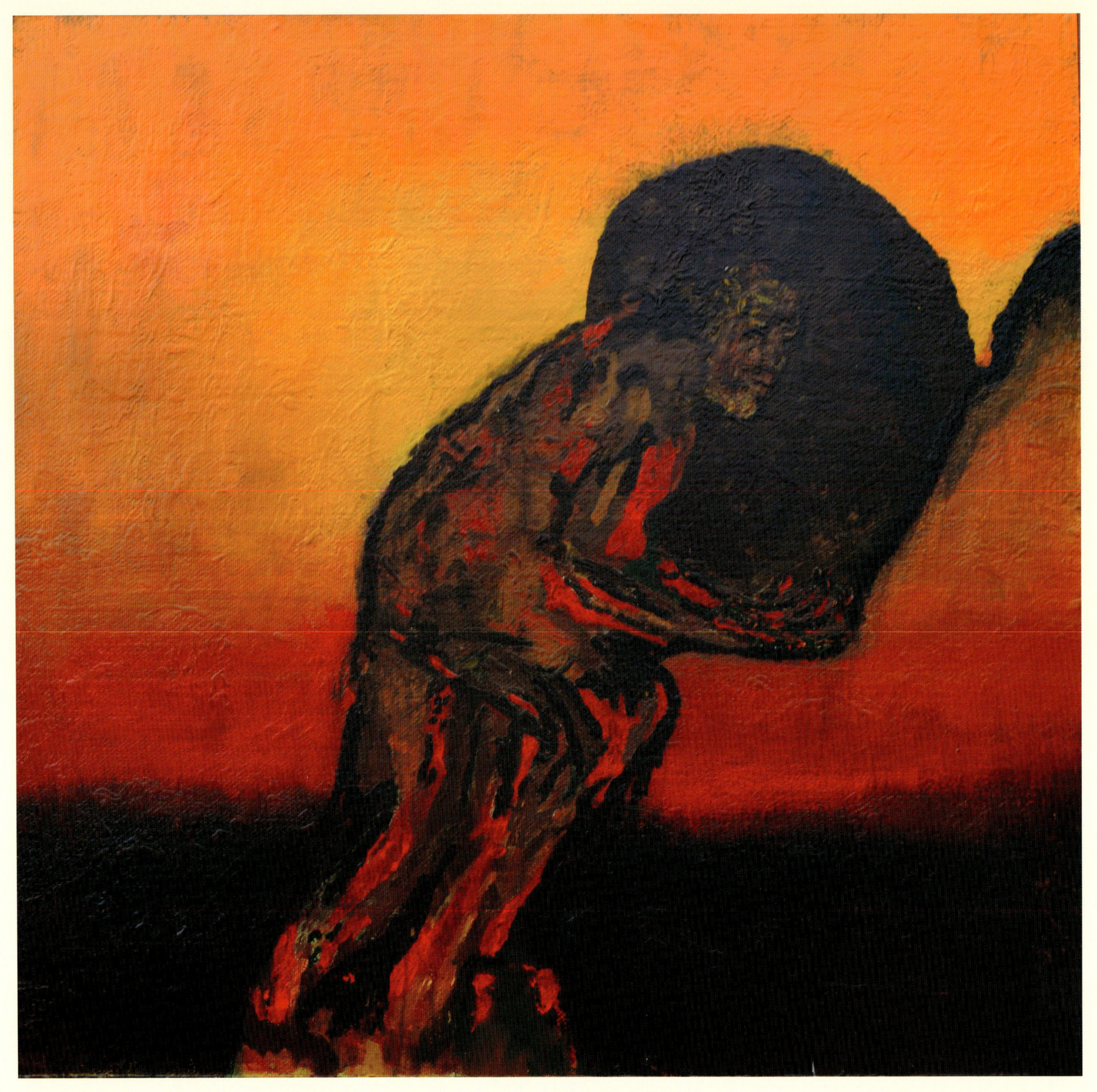

SISYPHUS

Acrylic on board
48" x 48"

Many of us spend time pursuing a dream, even getting close to achieving that dream,
only to experience our ambitions come tumbling down.

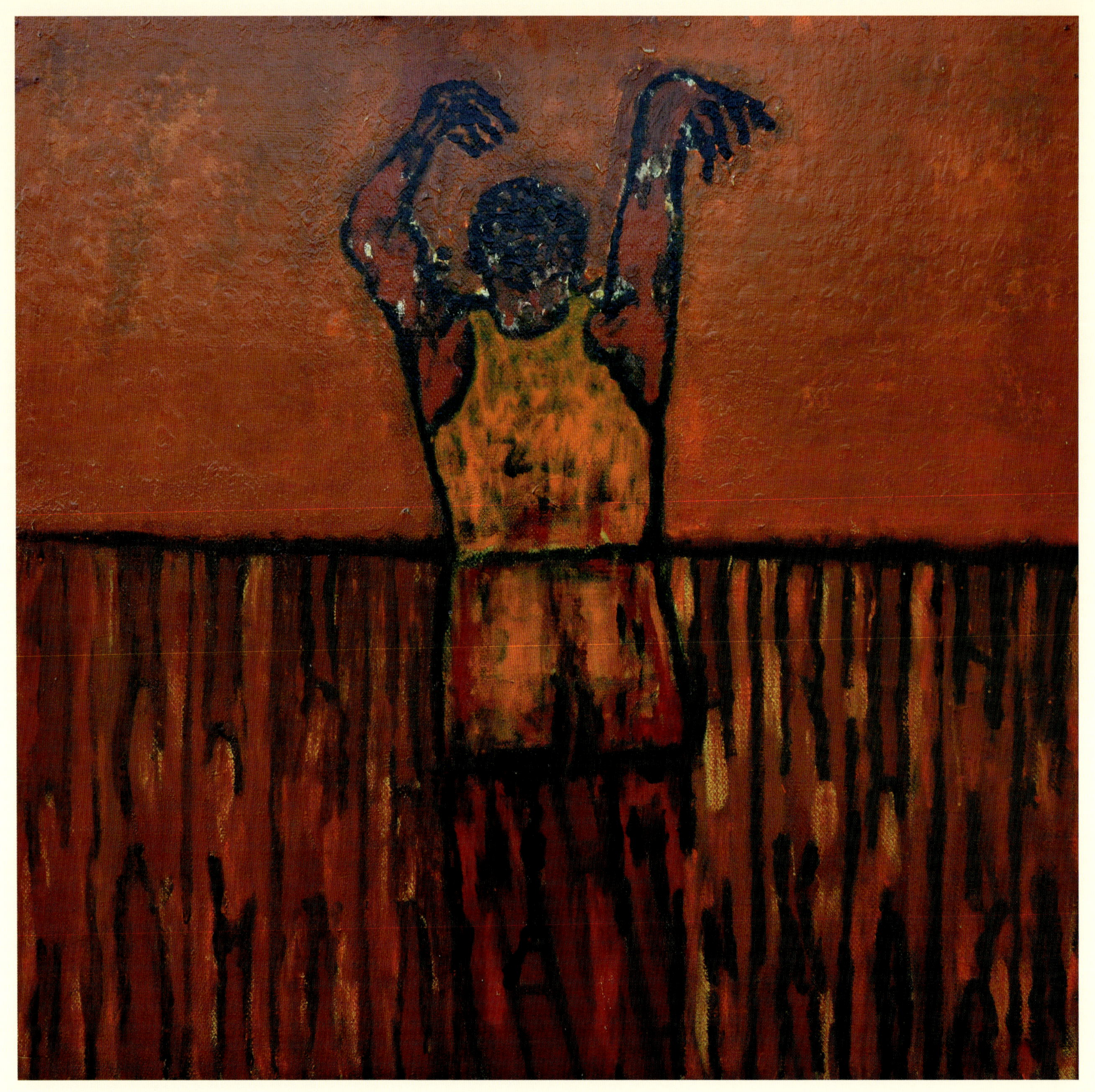

SHOOTER

Acrylic on board
48" x 48"

DON ARGEE BARKSDALE

Don Barksdale is part of that glorious cluster of the first black men to play in the National Basketball Association and to be inducted into the Naismith Memorial Basketball Hall of Fame. I met this smooth baritone long after his career had moved into the history books, while we were both living in the Bay Area in 1980. This giant of a man, thirty-five years my senior, was kind and generous to me. He always pulled for me in my "me against the world" battle that youngsters often embrace before the world tenderizes them. He even tried to persuade me to take up the good-walk-spoiled activity of golf. I think mostly it was just to have the opportunity during our golf outings to ease some of his wisdom and patience onto me.

I always looked forward to my fellowship with Don, though I never developed much patience or talent on the golf course. However, one day, out of nowhere, I leaned into that little white ball with all I had, and away it went for what felt like an eternity, until it landed on the other end of the world. Don was so proud and excited. During our manly fist-pumping and high-fiving, he kept repeating, "Kat, you really hit that ball! We better check to see if the cover is still on it."

My last conversation with him was from his hospital bed. We chatted, and he smiled as he returned to the subject of the distance that I hit that golf ball all those years ago: "Joe Barry, you remember when you hit that ball that day? Kat, you really hit that ball."

In memory of Don Argee Barksdale (1923-1993)

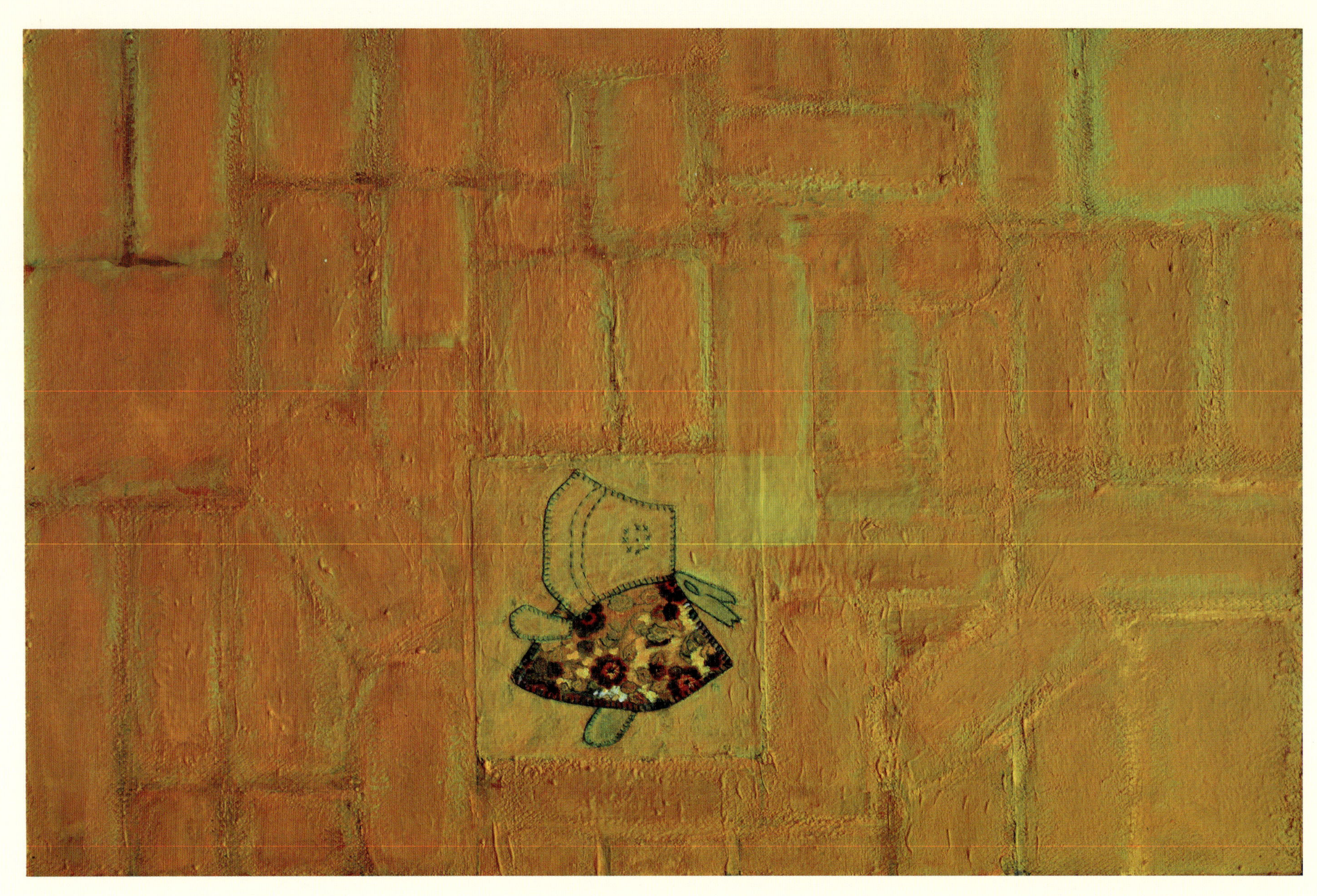

AMBER MAIDEN

Acrylic and mixed materials on board
48" x 32"

COBBLAH

This recipe was originally shared with me by a former girlfriend. I knew this woman for a long time, but this delicious dessert remains my favorite part of that relationship. Sad, but true. You have found me out—great food rules me. She introduced it as a cobbler, but historically, cobbler has been more a wonderful combination of dense, rich crust covered with ample butter, sugar, and peaches. This sweet thing right here is more like custard, pie, and sweetbread combined into one. I absolutely love this ridiculously wonderful, sweet and buttery thing. My favorite part of this deliciousness is that usually, I already have the ingredients required to prepare it.

Bottom

Half-Cup Olive Oil　　　　　　　　Half-Cup Butter　　　　　　　　Cup Chopped Pecans

Combine oil, butter, and chopped pecans in a glass baking dish.

Middle

Create a batter with:

Cup Flour　　　　　　　　Cup Sugar　　　　　　　　Cup Milk　　　　　　　　Teaspoon Baking Powder

Pour this batter over the oil, butter, and nut mixture.

Top

I have used many toppings with this recipe—canned, fresh, or overly ripened peaches, blueberries, and apples—but my most recent favorite topping is made with sweet potatoes. Prepare the following to pour on top:

Two Cups Chopped Sweet Potatoes　　　　　　　　Tablespoon Butter Flavor

Half-Cup Brown Sugar　　　　　　　　Two Tablespoons Vanilla Extract

Cup Water　　　　　　　　Tablespoon Cinnamon

Once everything has been put together, I allow the elements in my glass baking dish to settle into itself in the time needed for the oven to heat to 350 degrees. Bake for sixty minutes on the bottom oven rack. Allow to sit and cool.

For those who need to go all the way in, or, as they say, "if you cannot help yourself," this should be accompanied with a legal scoop of dulce de leche ice cream. For those pretending to be reasonable in the midst of this debauchery, your favorite coffee will do. The bittersweet nature of coffee offers a rich counterbalance to all the wonderfulness of this "cobbler." I suggest removing your shoes before you dive into this dessert. Bare feet add an additional layer of pleasure to decadence, because when the delight reaches your toes, you are free to wiggle.

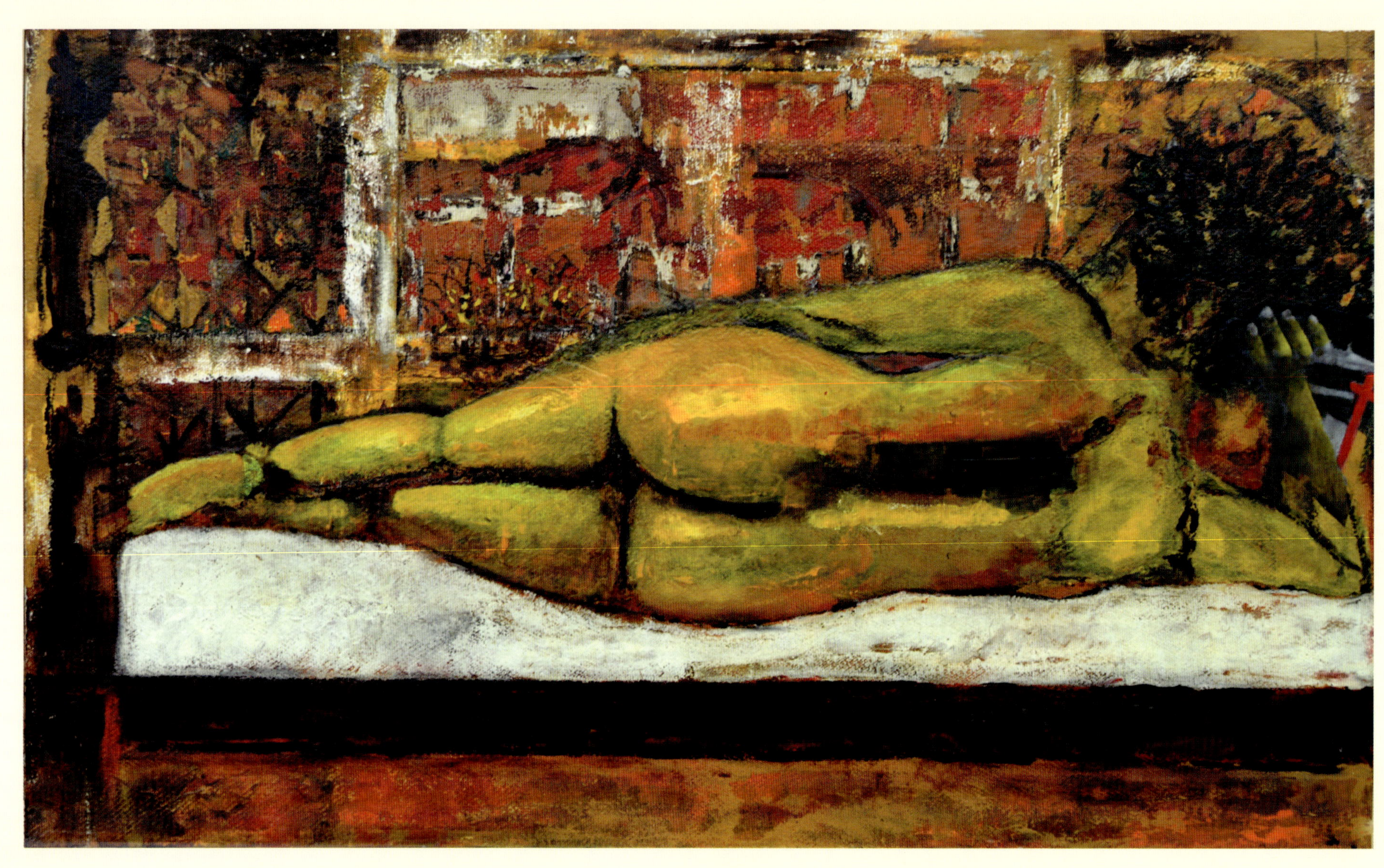

WOMAN

Acrylic and mixed materials on board
48" x 32"

FUNDAMENTAL

My desire and love for my woman are full and eternal. I am clear. I assume it is that way for other relationships as well, no matter how that composition shows up in the world, in all the varieties of human attractions.

I do not know why some of us are attracted to one person and not another or why we fall in love with this person and not that one. However, I have to believe that LGBTQIAP—Lesbian, Gay, Bisexual, Transgender, Queer, Intersex, Asexual, and Pansexual—people and all of their details are as natural and true to them as my life being a heterosexual male is natural and true to me.

If and when we have experienced joy and happiness for ourselves, we should want the same for others.

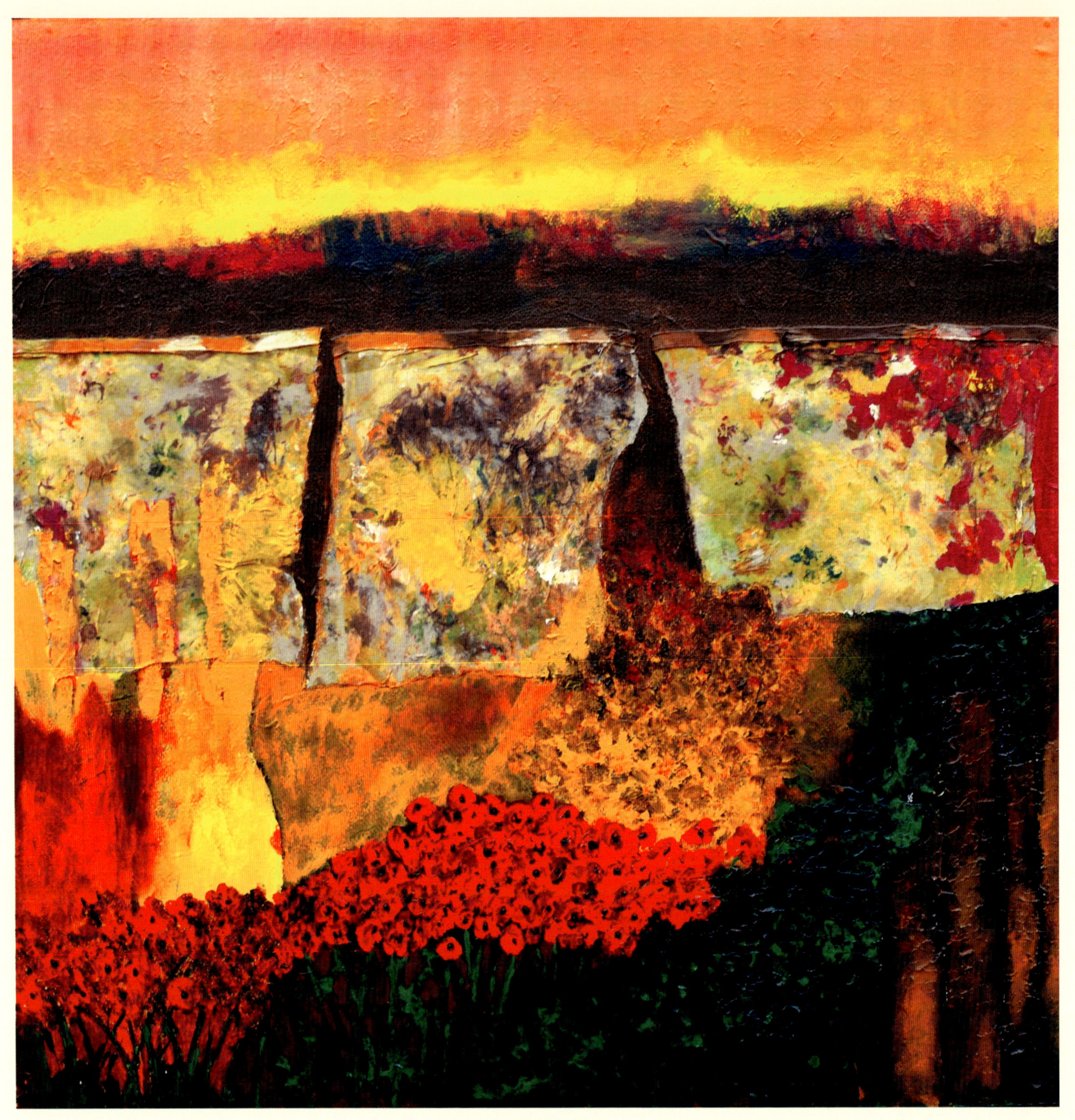

RAGS

Acrylic and mixed materials on board
48" x 48"

WRINGER

Among my memories of a time gone by, I recall my family washing clothes with the old-fashioned, wringer-style washing machine there on our back porch in my hometown of Pine Bluff, Arkansas. This raucous device had replaced the number-three metal-tub-and-washboard combination we had used before. While this contraption may have been just one step up from when cave people beat clothes on a rock in a nearby stream, we welcomed it as progress nonetheless.

After clothes were washed and then rinsed by the agitator in the tub below, we would pass each item, by hand, one-by-one, through the two rollers above the tub that would squeeze water from the clothing, bedding, and such. After clothes were hung to be dried outside on a line, you had to prop that sagging line up with a long stick to protect your handiwork from dragging in the dirt or having it become undone by wandering dogs as you waited on what hopefully would be a warm, sunny day. At day's end, as we retrieved each dried item from the clothesline, we would once again discover that wonderful scent of fresh air and sunshine bound up in our laundry as a reward for all of our efforts. It was the scent of everything that was beautiful from nature and what was right in the world.

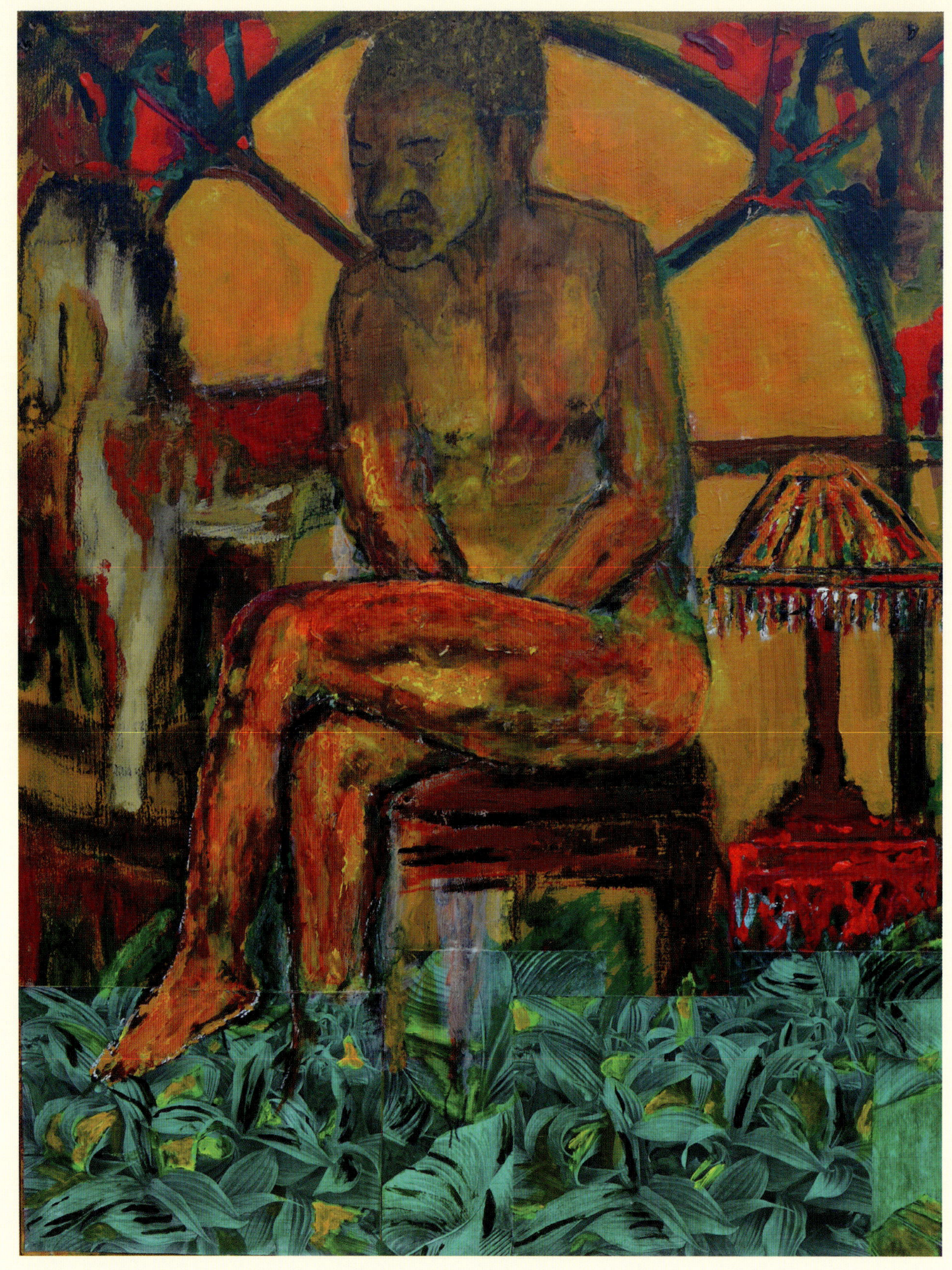

GARDEN

Acrylic and mixed materials on board
32" x 48"

A SPECIAL PLACE

We should be careful in all of our providing for others that we do not fail to get something for ourselves. Each of us needs some thing or some place that we retreat to for personal nurturing and sustenance. We owe it to ourselves to carve out that special place just for ourselves. This special place may be different things for different people, but everyone needs it—something as simple as powering off the phone, sitting in quiet, taking a long walk, dancing when no one is watching, singing along with a favorite song, or experiencing any of your favorite things in solitude.

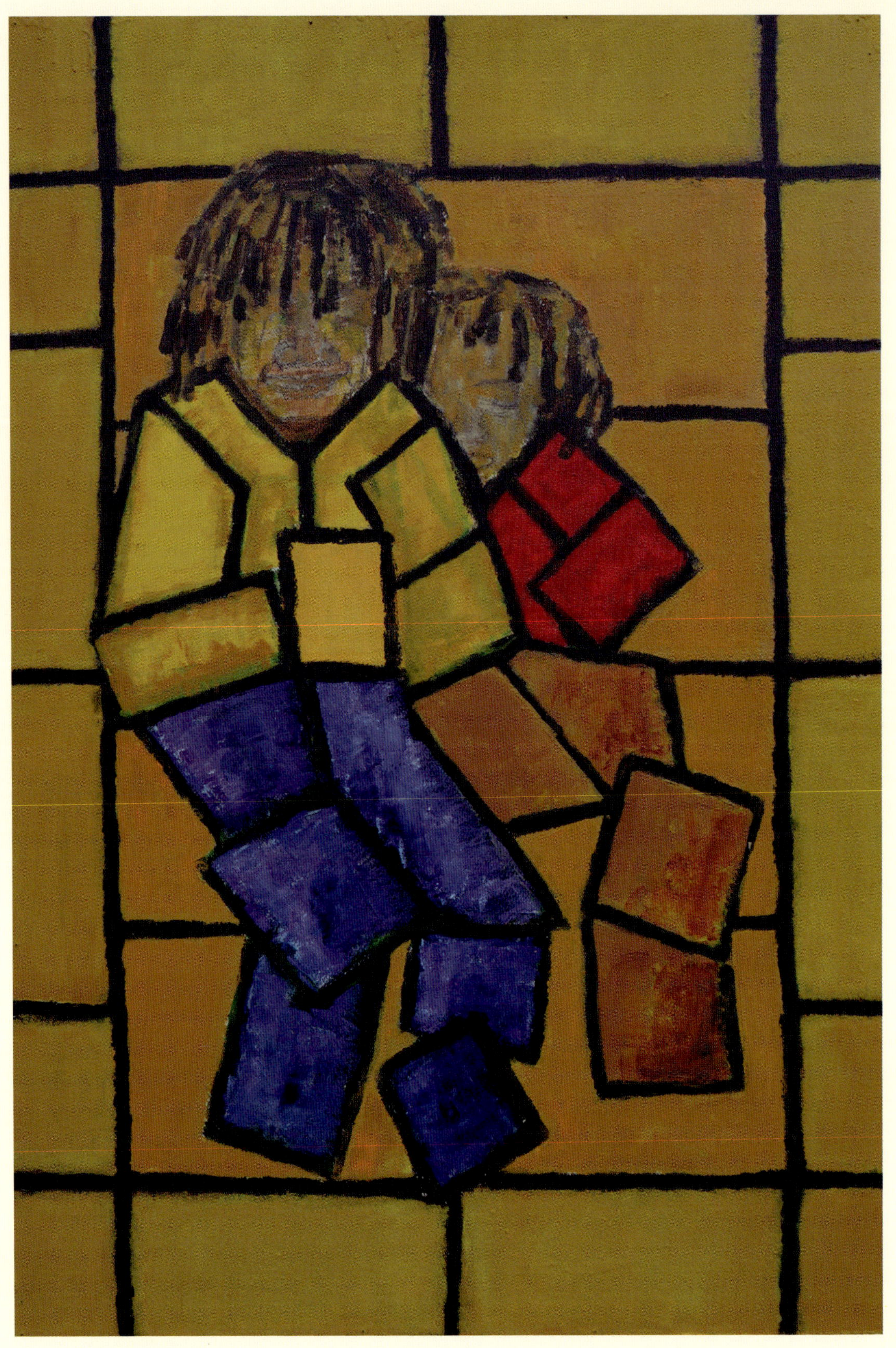

BRUH

Acrylic on board
32" x 48"

BIG BROTHERS

The person I refer to as my big brother is not bigger than me, he is simply older. Saying "big brother" is a nod of deference. I am much like many other younger brothers throughout the world who admired their older brother. He always seemed to be faster, smarter, more handsome, and more interesting than anyone else I knew when I was a little boy.

In his heart, my big brother wanted us to be straight out of a Norman Rockwell painting full of kites, baseball, bubble gum, and swimming pools. In reality, he was just too busy. He was always on the run—running after this, running after that. I remember most about him that he was always headed out the back door or asleep, recovering from all that he did when out in the world. I never seemed to gain his undivided attention in the way that little brothers crave from their big brothers.

I always felt that my brother would do better if he could. He has good intentions, but it is sometimes hard for him to do the good that he intends. Always so self-involved, he just could not stop himself. It seems that motion is the instrument of the ambitious. I wonder if the folk of his tribe ever find what they are looking for and if there will ever be enough of what they seek, even if they find it. It seems that their craving for this elusive thing is insatiable. Their desires can be fed but never satisfied.

I remember being impressed that as a teenager, he made his way backstage at an Otis Redding concert, or at least I recall he said he did, and that is enough for a little brother listening to the tales of his big brother. He shared with me in later years that it was actually James Brown he saw in person; James Brown, Otis Redding, Superman, or a unicorn—everything is believable to a young boy listening to tales, real and imagined, of his older brother.

Perhaps it is the little things that matter after all. For all of my brother's proud boasts and bravado, what I remember most is that he gave me a hardback edition of poems by Countee Cullen for my high school graduation. I want to think that his gift of this book to me meant that my big brother understood something about me after all. And he once took me to the racetrack and paid for my burrito.

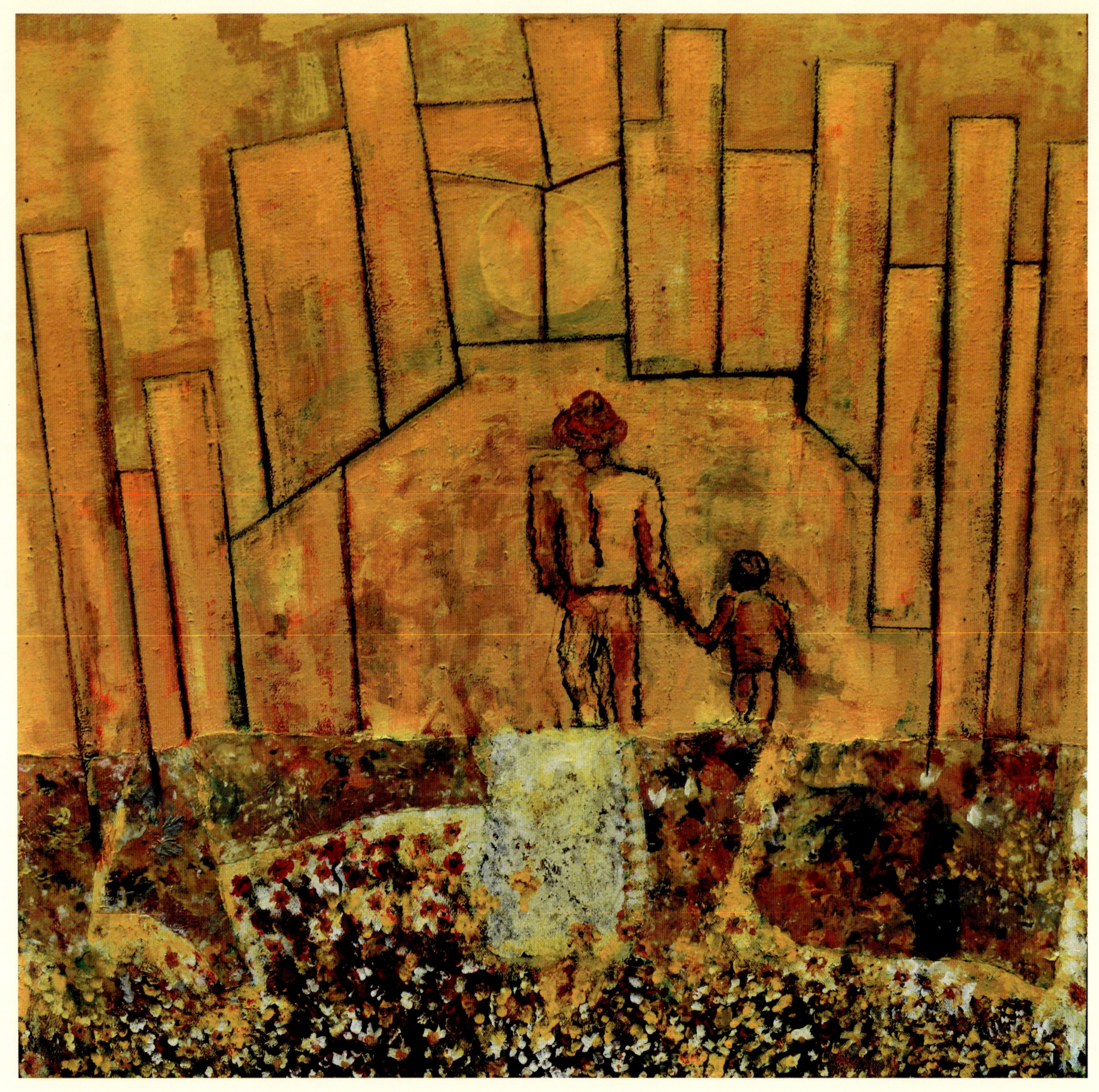

HATS

Acrylic and mixed materials on board
48" x 48"

HE AND HIS SHADOW

Daddy had a perfect sense of fashion for himself, as he wore fine suits and was well-groomed. He did not, however, quite get the detail of what was appropriately stylish for a child to wear. If he bought himself a fedora-style hat, I was in line to receive one as well. I would probably have been better served to have a baseball cap, like most children my age, yet there I was, a miniature version of my father. We were such a sight together, we two: He had a hat; I had a hat. He had dark glasses; I had dark glasses. Once, someone who did not know any better wondered who was this blind man in the dark glasses being led around by a young boy. My father was not blind, and I was not leading him anywhere; he was simply holding my hand as we went from place to place.

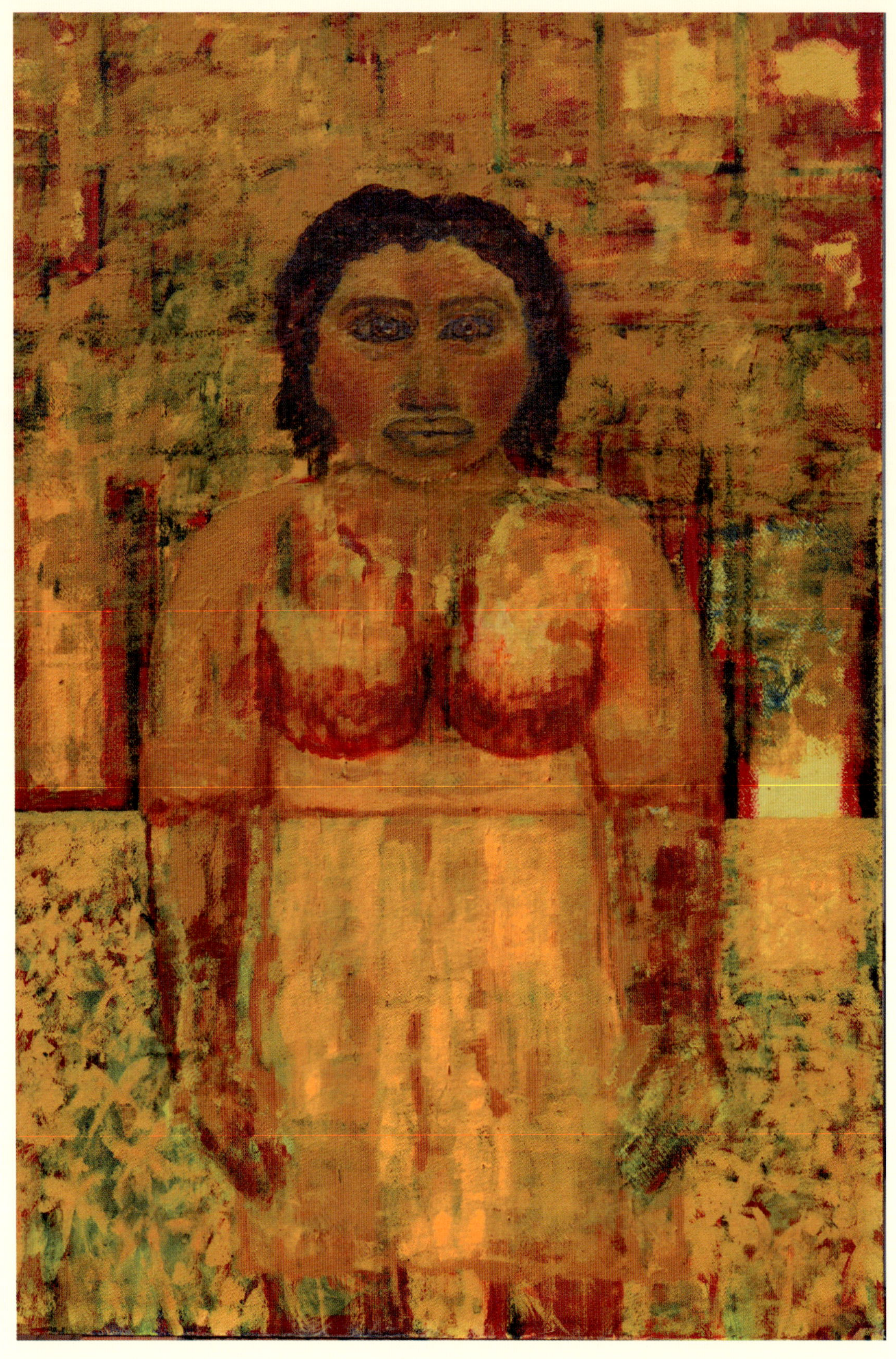

MAE

Acrylic on board
32" x 48"

A FRIEND

I met her when we were young—full of ambition and requirement. We now find ourselves all "growed up" and on the other side of life's harsh realities, which for her include a double mastectomy and chemotherapy.

My friend of all these years called to say she wanted me to take her to the store, so I did, because that is what friends do in this season of our lives. It didn't really matter that I could have easily just picked up the items for her, or even had them delivered. That would have been what I wanted, not what and how she wanted it for herself. What seemed most important to my dear friend was that I drive the distance and make the effort required, so I did. Most often, it was easier to just give this very successful and highly accomplished woman what she wanted, instead of bearing witness to her pouting with pretty lips poked out. I chose to indulge my friend, who at times appeared to be a full-grown woman wrapped in a little girl's emotions. I made the forty-five-minute drive to where she lived and then took her to the store.

As we were returning from our errand, she asked if I wanted ice cream. I did not, but I sensed that the question was really a request for the ice cream that she wanted. So, there we were, pulling away from the drive-through with a small oxygen tank by her side and two very tall strawberry milkshakes in tow. Upon returning to her home, I unloaded everything and joined her there in the backyard on a very warm summer day. Words were of little use as we sat in communion, in the shade, with our ice cream and silence.

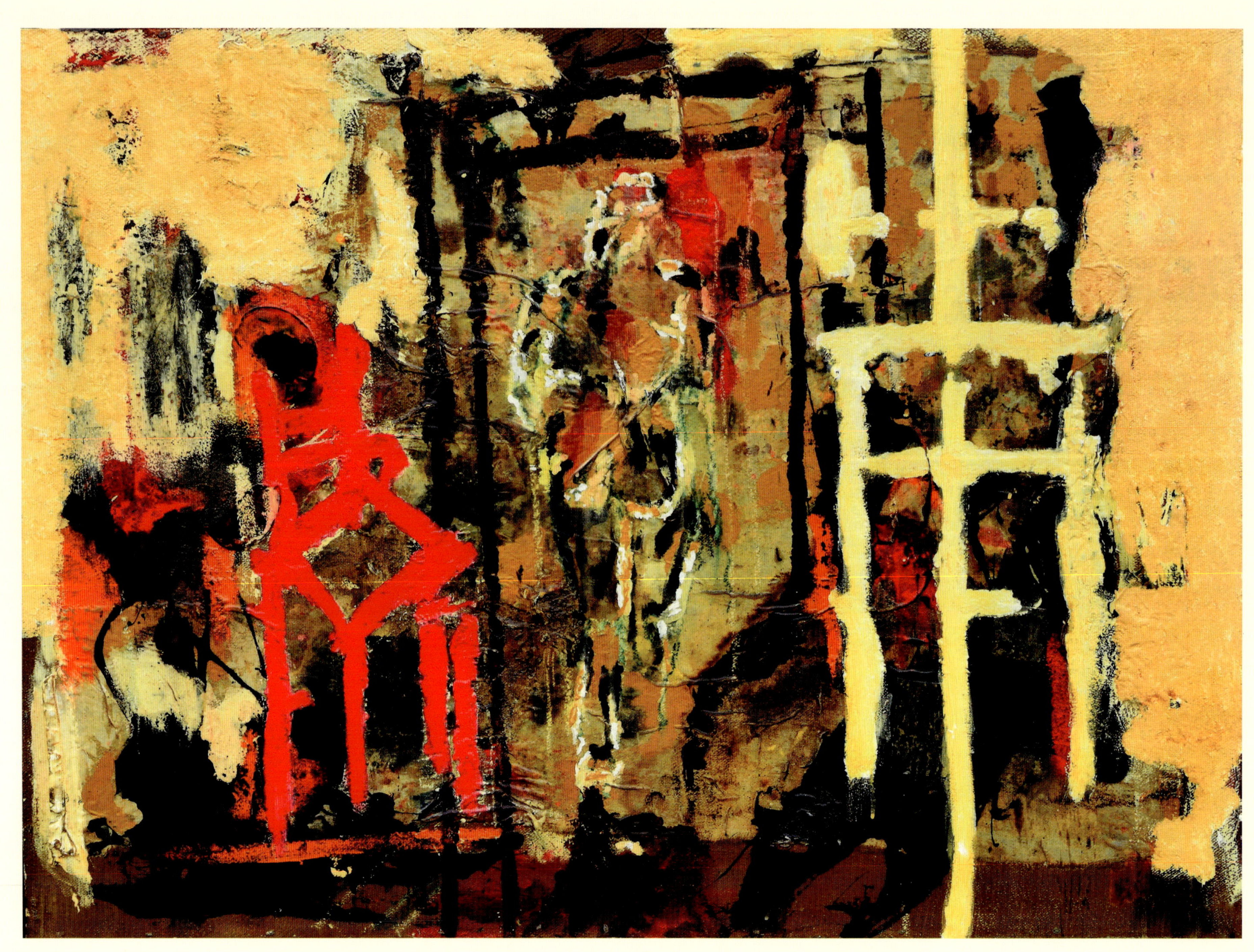

MOVE

Acrylic on board
48" x 32"

MOTION AS MEDICINE

The world can be a tough place to be somebody. I am sensitive to how all the hurt, injury, and disappointment the world throws at us can tempt some folks to sit down and not get back up again. That, however, does not work for me. I have to keep moving!

I doubt that I can forget my mistakes, and I do not want to forget my victories, but come what may, I need to move forward.

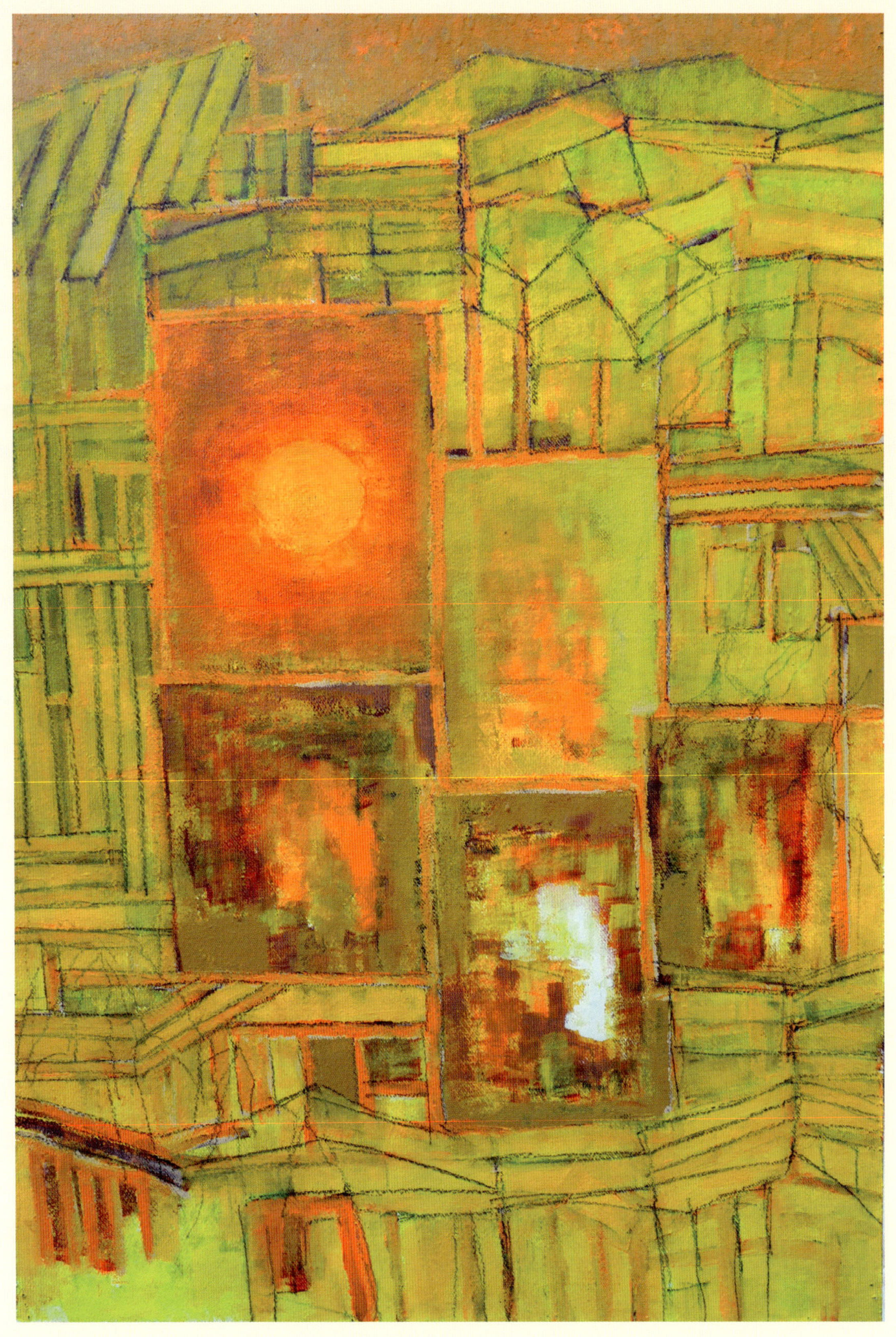

FAVELA

Acrylic on board
32" x 48"

A PLEA

I grew up very poor. I witnessed the struggle of my parents and other members of my family working very hard, every day, yet having very little to show for it. We were members of the segment of society that is the working poor.

I remain hopeful that as a society, we will move to solve for the lack of food, shelter, education, and healthcare. Anything less is immoral and vulgar. I believe that it is only when people are properly nourished, educated, and healthy that we can truly expect anything reasonable from them. How can a malnourished, undereducated, sick person properly function in a civilized society? Hunger, undereducation, and poor health make a person feeble and alter their better judgment and productivity. They do the best they can, but that is not the same thing as doing their very best.

I am confounded as to why America chooses not to properly address poverty even though we have the resources and knowledge to bring people above the poverty line. Perhaps there is a fear by some that lending aid to the poor and dispossessed is giving them something for free, while others are earning it the hard way. I disagree. Many families that accept aid do so for food and healthcare for their children. Those are not luxuries. Trust and believe, "them that got" are not going to lose ground by being humane and compassionate to very poor families. As stakeholders in this society, our own quality of life is actually improved by ensuring the fundamentals of food, shelter, education, and healthcare for everyone in desperate need. The call of a civilized and moral society is to do for "the least of these."

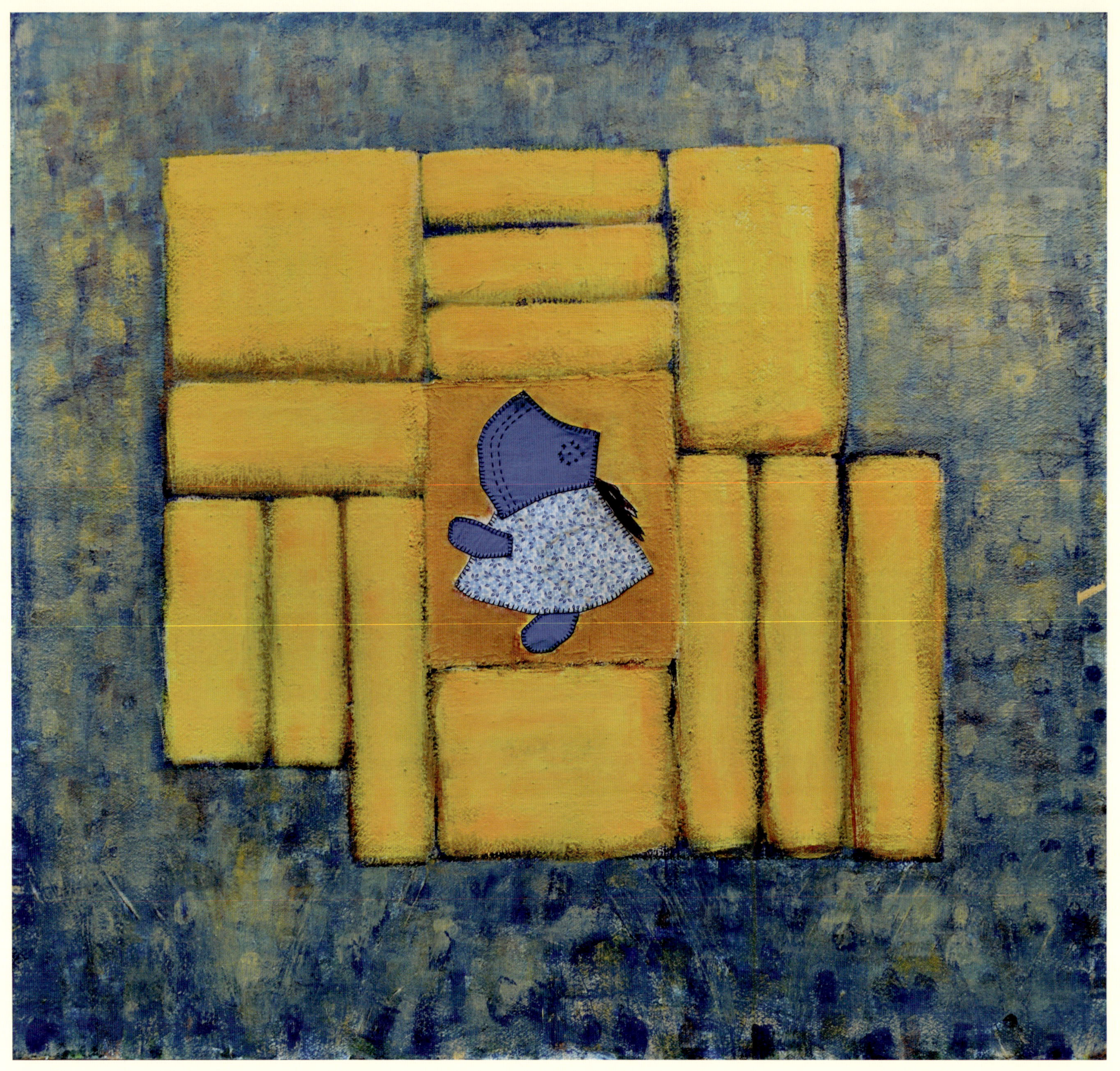

BLUE MAIDEN

Acrylic and mixed materials on board
48" x 48"

SEA BASS

This preparation is excellent for most fish, but is ideal for sea bass.

Sea Bass Fillets	Black Pepper
Egg Whites	Salt
Onion Powder	Panko Crumbs, unseasoned

Dust sea bass with ample onion powder, pepper and salt to taste or physician's orders. Drench in egg whites. Cover with panko crumbs. Allow to sit for the time it takes to heat your favorite skillet to medium. Add just enough oil to cover the base of the skillet but not too much, because this is more a sauté, not a deep fry. Depending on the thickness of the bass fillet, I cook this similar to the way I cook a hamburger—three minutes, more or less, on each side. Turn the fire off and allow this delicious fish to sit. I enjoy this rich, flaky fish with a crisp potato or lentils, something that will provide a texture to move against the delicate nature of sea bass. As for wine, I prefer a Chardonnay or a Sauvignon Blanc blend.

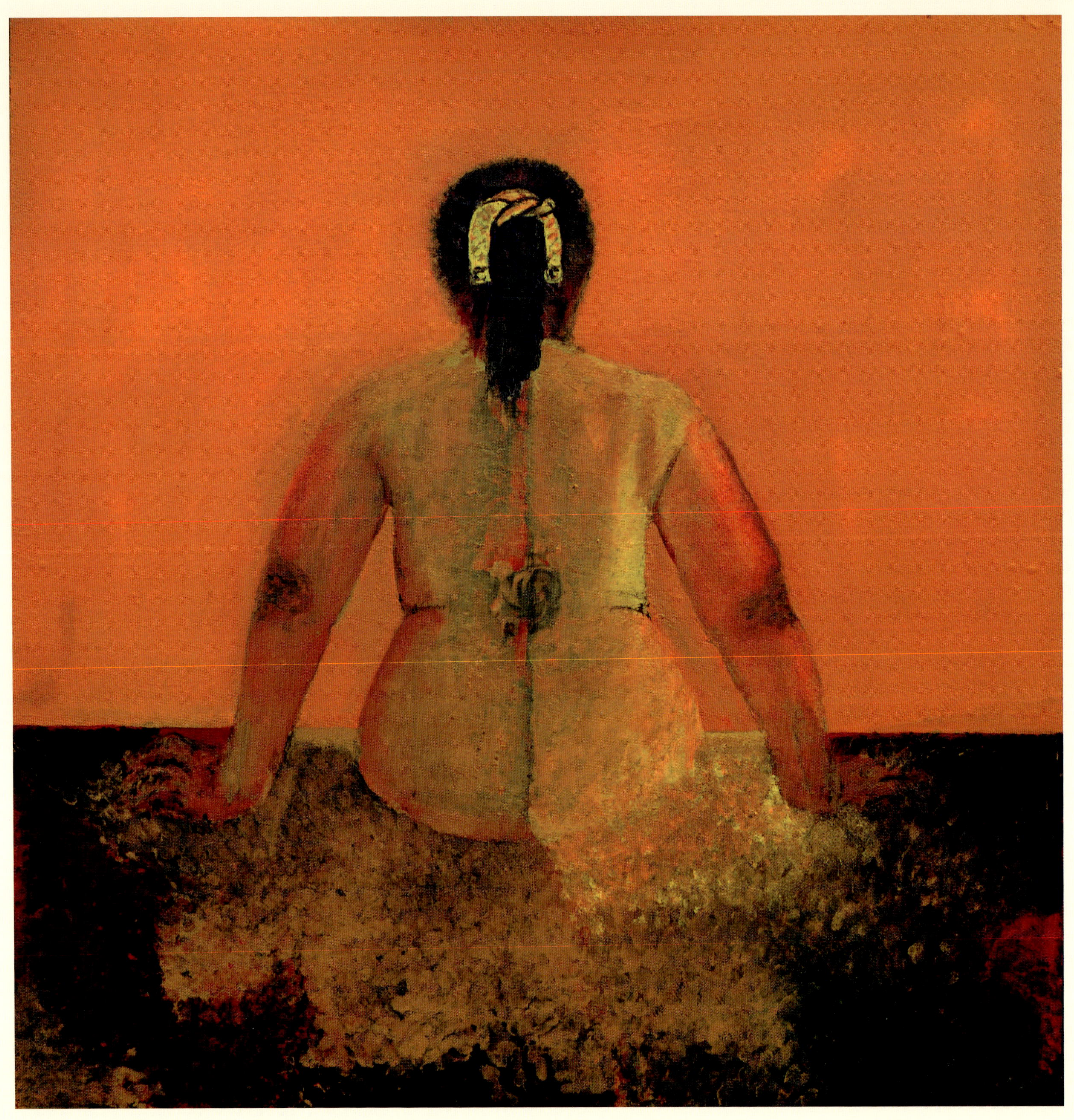

ROSE

Acrylic on board
48" x 48"

HER REALITY

In a time gone by, I was in the midst of complimenting a very successful and talented friend on just how impressive she was. The response of this smart, wealthy, and capable person gave me pause. While flattered by my observation, she nonetheless shared her own unfiltered reflection of how she gets up each morning shaking in her boots of uncertainty, never knowing if this is the day that everything will come tumbling down. She offered that she could never be certain if she would be predator or prey in our jungle of humanity. Each day in the jungle, one animal must outrun the other to survive. One is in search of food, and the other is hoping to not be that food.

Everyone, everywhere maintains a little of that fear and uncertainty within them. Our egos engage in such a way that denies us from disclosing just how vulnerable we feel from time to time, but there is always something there to remind us.

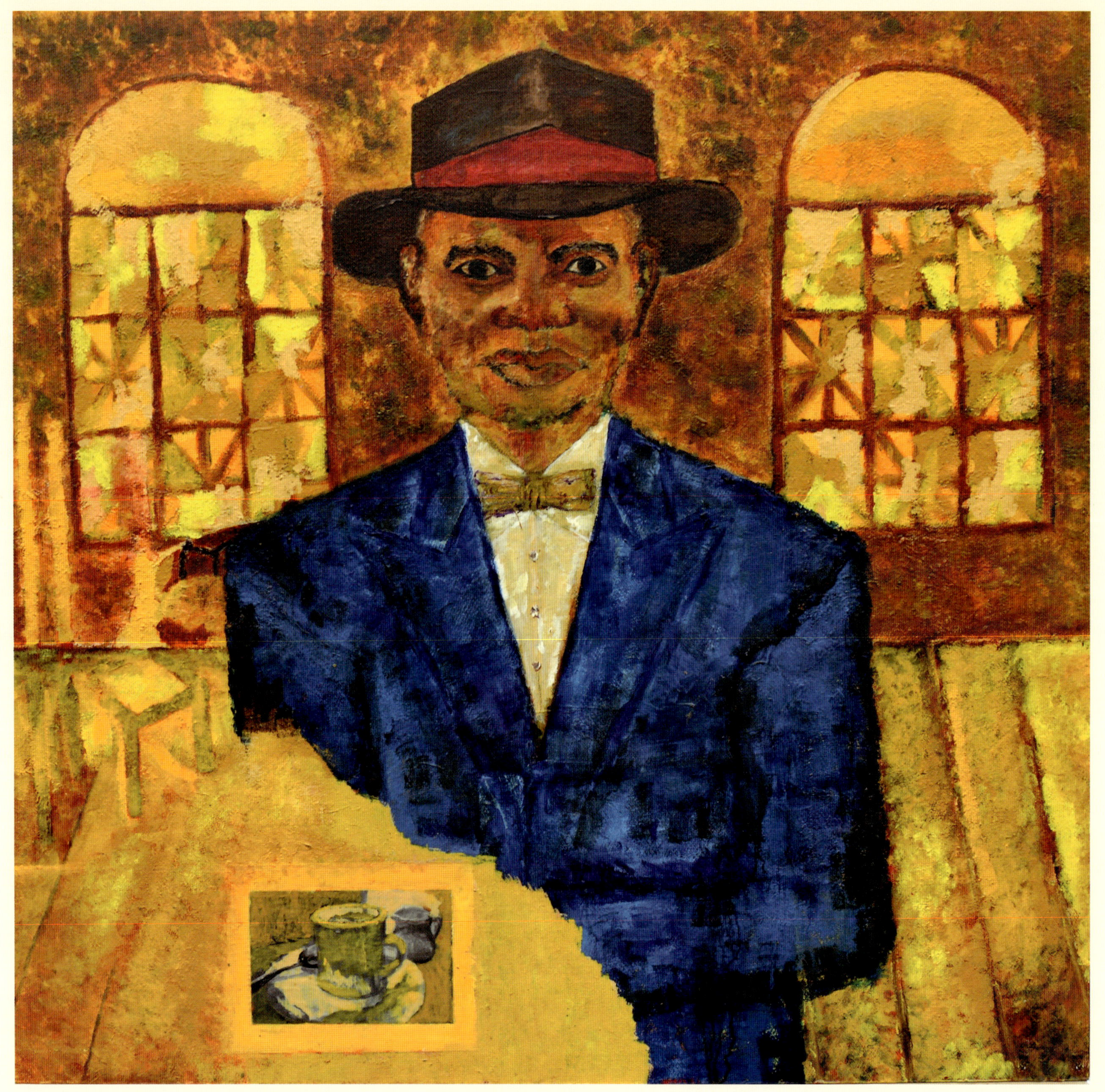

MISTAGEORGE

Acrylic and mixed materials on board
48" x 48"

COFFEE CUPS

Mr. George was our family friend from long ago. I remember him seated there at our kitchen table, having coffee with Momma. Wearing a suit and tie, with felt hat nearby, he seemed on his way to someplace or stopping by as he made his way home. Mr. George worked at 1960s Pine Bluff Arsenal, so it is safe to assume that his regular work routine did not involve a suit and tie. Looking back, I assume that dressing up was his treat to himself. My mother would piddle around her kitchen as Mr. George would tell her where he had been and what he had seen.

He was always kind and generous to us children. In addition to his engaging personality, he gave us enough pocket change to get cookies and penny candy at B.W. Jones Corner Store. Sometimes, he would reach deep into his trouser pocket and return with a handful of coins that he would gently place on the table for whichever of us children were lucky enough to be present.

In those times, if Mr. George had his fill of spirits before his ritual cup of coffee with my mother, he would entertain us. He had this charming rambling that he performed that could have easily been lyrics to any Southern blues record. He would tell my mother (whose name is Annie Mae) in a blues man's cadence, "Baby, I think I love you, cause your name is Annie Mae." He rhymed it like he meant it, but my mother would usually dismiss his flirtations, though not so much as to discourage him from coming around for his next cup of coffee.

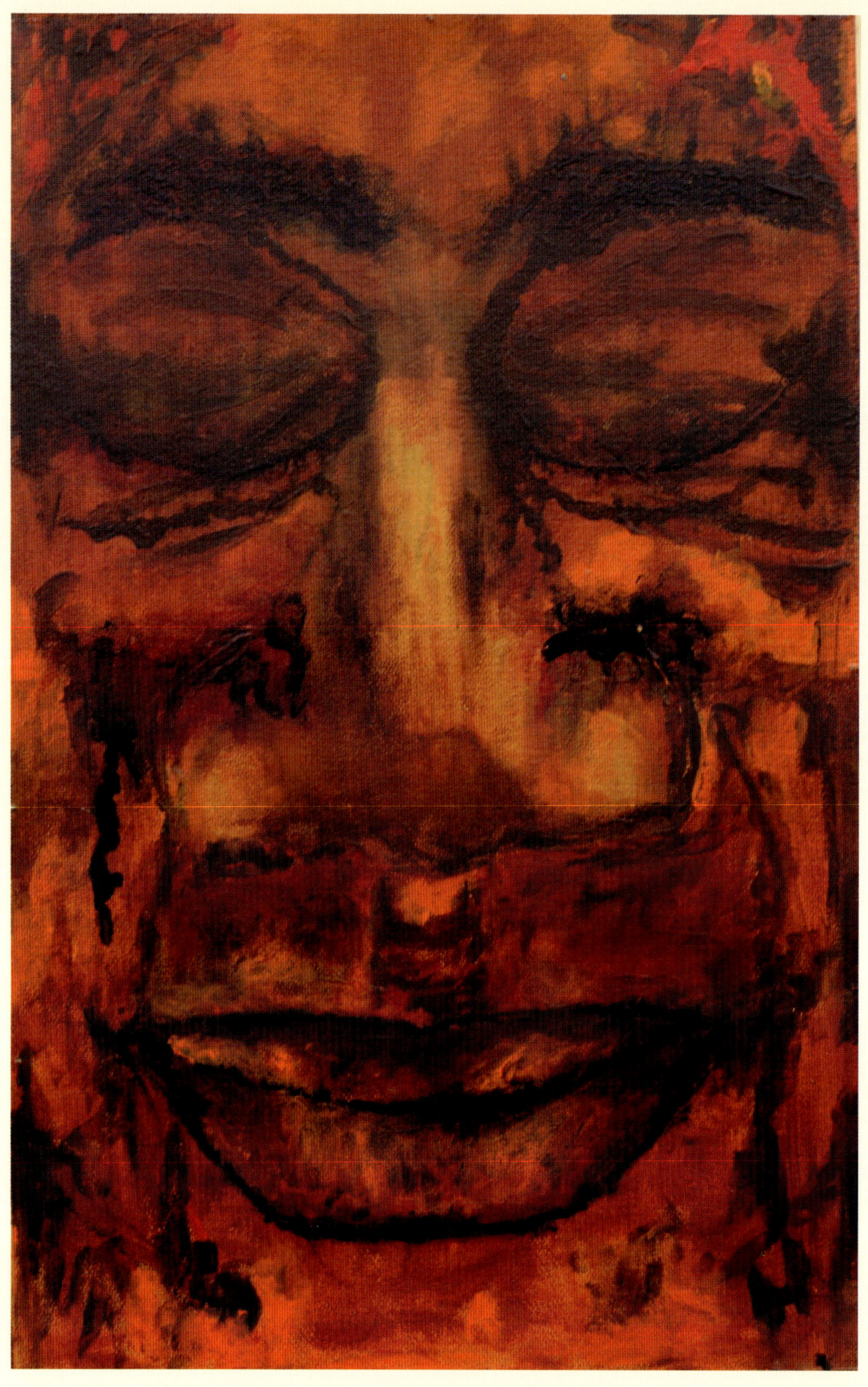

SELF PORTRAIT

Acrylic and mixed materials on board
32" x 48"

CONTRITE

Let me at thy throne of mercy
Find a sweet relief;
Kneeling there in deep contrition,
help my unbelief.
—Crosby

To the extent that I do believe in God, I believe God to be inseparable from all living things, large and small. God is in everything, every place, all the time. God is not isolated and separated from us, out there or up in the clouds. This theology of the inseparability of God and God's creations moves me to be kind to my neighbor to the extent that my human imperfection will allow. Compassion, kindness, and benevolence are also fundamental in the composition of who I would have God be.

Much of our lives is spent making peace with how we feel about religion, spirituality, and God. While we may identify with the general thesis of a specific religion, as we add our own details and exceptions to religious doctrine, we ultimately arrive at our very own self-prescribed theology. What may have sprung out of good intentions often morphs into something else, individually tailored by each user.

These customized theologies become evident in the images that the faithful present of their Creator, often resembling who they would have God be if they had created God or who God would be if they were God. I am unable to accept that God is all-powerful, yet lacking benevolence, or that the most-high and brilliant God is at the same time jealous and requiring of ritualistic worship. It is unbelievable to me that this genius Creator would be saddled with the traits of mere mortals. It feels to me that religion may even become weaponized in some ways—alternately a sword to assault thine enemy and a shield used for protection and comfort in this rough-and-tumble world.

Although, there is at least one hitch to my resistance to conventional religion and the concept of Heaven and hell. If I am wrong and God really is up in those clouds micromanaging all of this grand creation, and there really is a Heaven and hell, then I could potentially be in trouble come Judgment Day. Especially if God is confirmed to be that Old Testament variety who smites, hexes, and performs damnations on alternating days. However, I believe in a God who will be forgiving on the day that I appear for my ultimate and final judgment. I really do not believe that Heaven is so full that it will not accept me because I may have been inclined not to do the good I should and sometimes did what I should not. After all, isn't it God who made me that way? Amen.

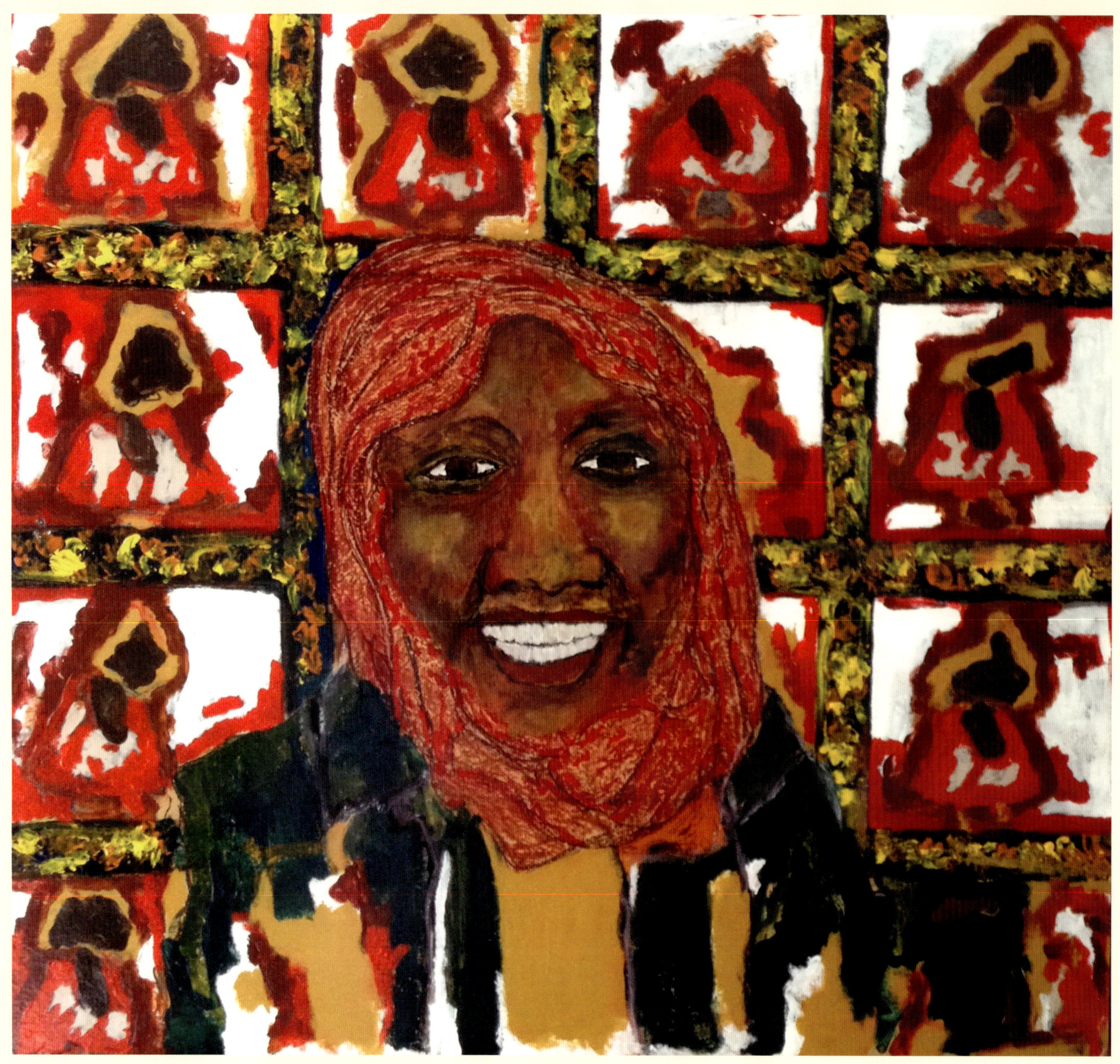

ARIE

Acrylic on board
48" x 48"

FAMILY VALUE

No family is perfect; never has been and never will be—there are just too many moving parts. However, for better or worse, we need our family in ways that none of us can fully know or understand. Family life and culture is forever under construction. It can be complicated and almost impossible at times. As family members, we engage in mutual disappointment. I am disappointing my family at a rate equal to their disappointing me.

If need be, along the way we may even need to take a time-out from family dysfunction. A time-out and maybe time away, but we should never declare our blood relations to be over, final, and forever severed. Never say or do in the heat of anger what you will likely want to take back in the cool of another time. Come what may, reserve a place to land that will deliver you back to your tribe.

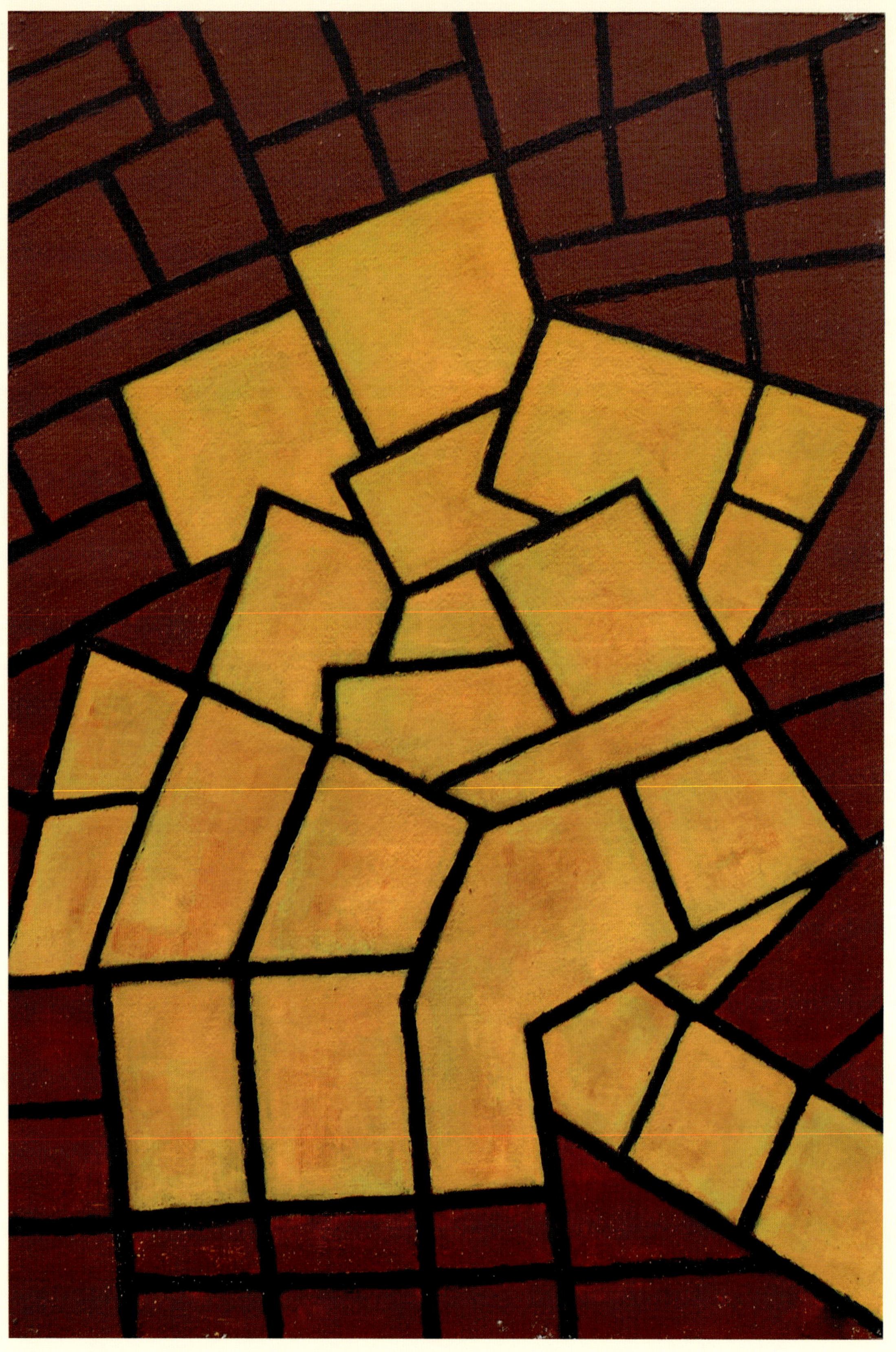

PO'

Acrylic on board
32" x 48"

SOLUTIONS

Somewhere along the way, it was determined that in order for the poor and dispossessed to get out of their predicament, they must become entrepreneurs. It is shortsighted and naive to think that owning a business will be the answer for everyone. I generally accept that everything is not for everybody, and there is more than one path to follow.

There is a place for those who can successfully build a career working for someone else directly, just as there is a place for entrepreneurship. Over these many years, I have created for-profit and nonprofit entities with mixed results. I enjoy the process, the creativity, the drama, and the rewards. However, it is important to note that becoming an entrepreneur does not guarantee stability, or success, and it most certainly doesn't assure riches.

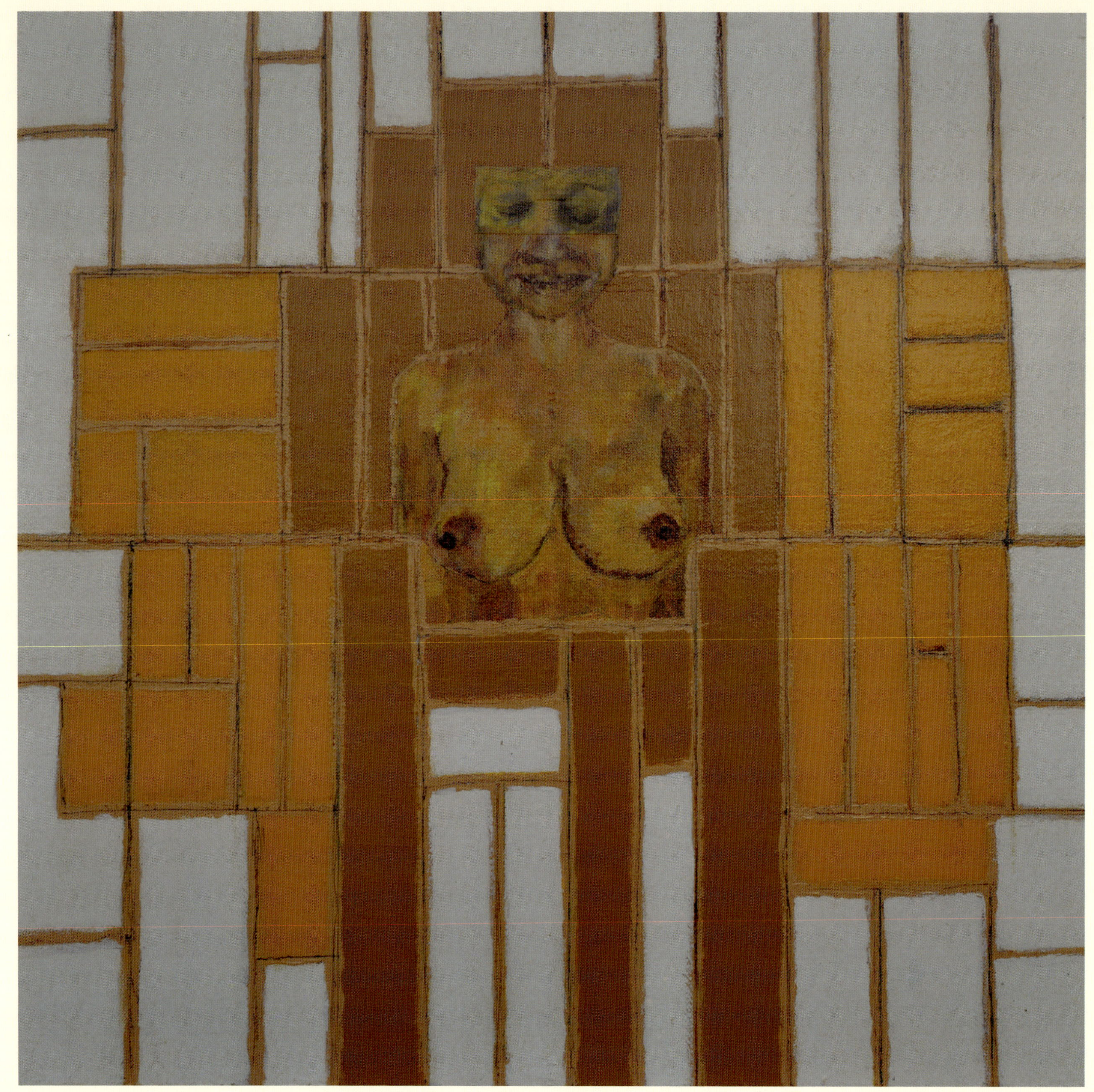

TRISHA

Acrylic and mixed materials on board
32" x 48"

COMING HOME

I ran into Trisha, an old friend, just the other day. She gave me one of those hugs as if I had just returned from the war. We had dated long ago but somehow lost touch along the way. She stood there with a hand on her hip as we took inventory of the sixty-year-old versions of ourselves. Trisha remained as vibrant and beautiful as I remember her from a time gone by. As we moved beyond nervous chatter, I introduced her to my woman, and she in turn introduced me to her wife. After a life of dating men, and a first marriage that had produced a now-grown daughter, Trisha was looking at her wife with the satisfaction that lies in truth. I did not ask into whether she identified herself as lesbian, bisexual, or pansexual; it mattered only that she was happy. We then said our goodbyes and headed out to resume our journey in the world.

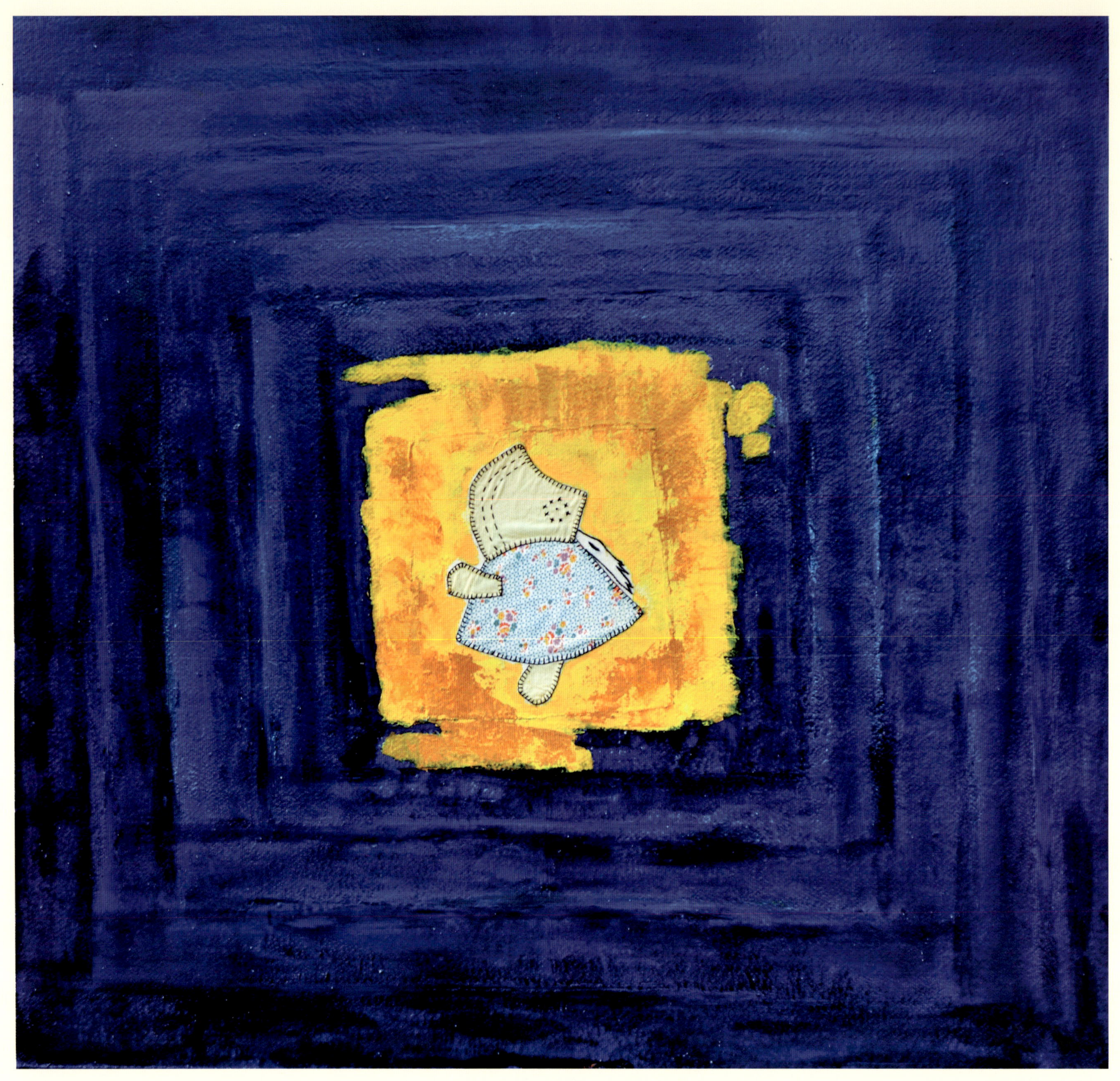

INDIGO MAIDEN

Acrylic and mixed materials on board
48" x 48"

SEAFOOD STEW

This gumbo-inspired recipe comes in two parts. Part one is the roux, which sets me up to layer in everything else. Now, I know there are aficionados who will argue whether this is gumbo or not. I can only offer that you are gonna waste time debating when you could be digging in to delicious.

Roux:

Half-Cup Oil

Half-Cup Flour

Fold equal parts oil and flour into your favorite heavy, large pot, slow and steady over medium-low heat until golden-brown with a consistency of gravy.

Add:

Two Cups Cooked Sausage	Two Cups Chopped Celery
Two Cups Chopped Cooked Chicken Thighs	Half-Tablespoon Red Pepper Flakes
Two Cups Lump Crab Meat	Half-Tablespoon Cayenne Pepper
Two Cups Shrimp	Two Tablespoons Vinegar
Two Cups Chopped Seared Okra	Quarter-Cup Celery Seed
Two Cups Chopped Tomatoes	Two Tablespoons Black Pepper
Half-Cup Chopped Garlic	Quarter-Cup Onion Powder
Two Cups Chopped Whole Onion	Quarter-Cup Garlic Powder

Cook at medium-low heat for half an hour. Lower heat to simmer for another half-hour, then allow to rest.

Brown rice may be better for us, but I prefer this composition served with white rice. For the truly inspired, I recommend this stew with your favorite cornbread. For those so inclined to the grape, perhaps your favorite Pinot Noir, as well. All of that pepper and spice in the stew plays well with the dark berries of the Pinot.

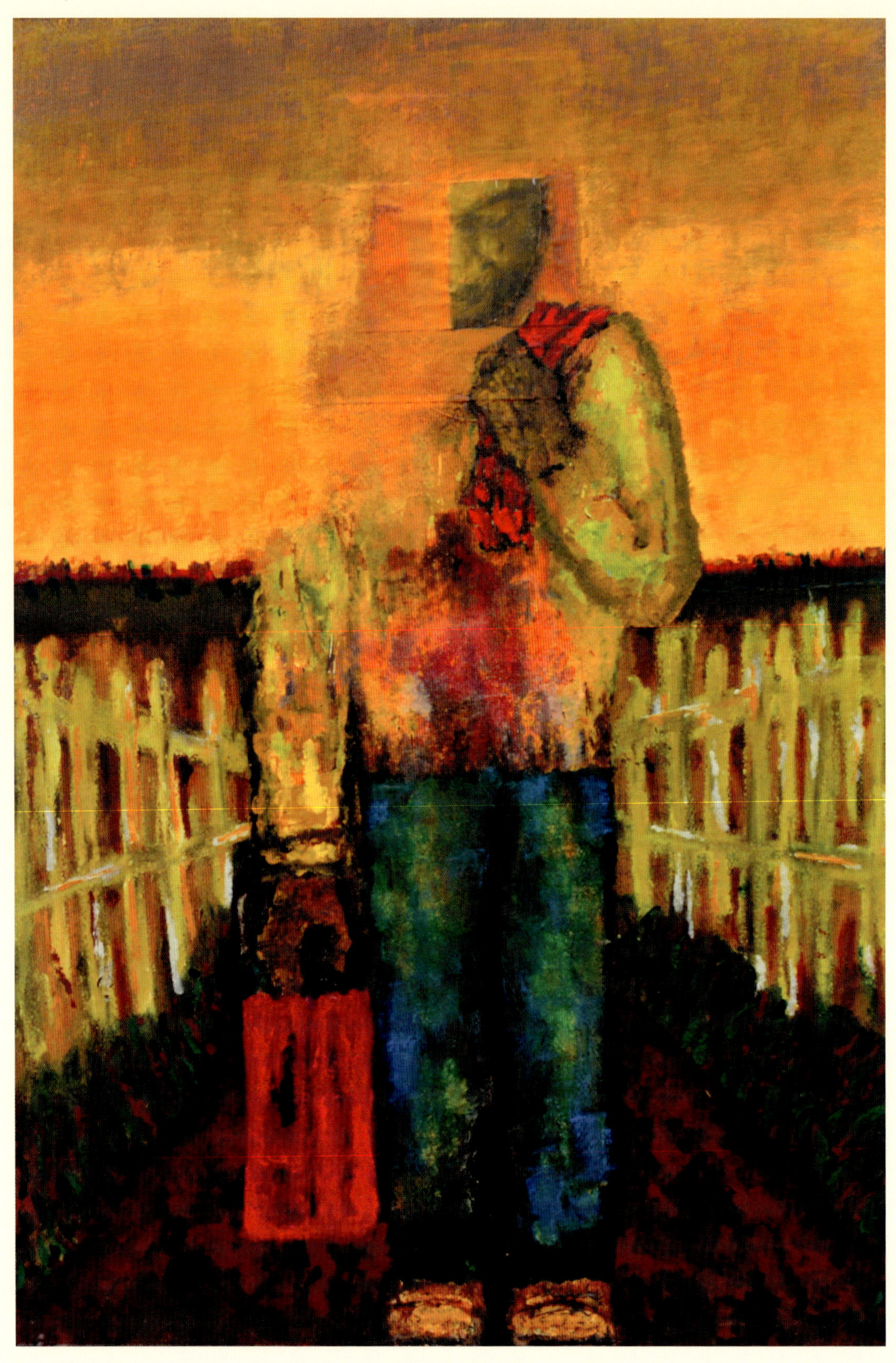

NOMAD

Acrylic and mixed materials on board
32" x 48"

WANDER

I visited Israel in 2013 along with other former NBA players on a goodwill tour. We were all part of an effort to bring Palestinian and Israeli children together under the umbrella of basketball. I doubt that sport alone will solve the deep and historical issues that are embedded in this region, but for a moment, we all gathered together for a traditional meal that signaled the conclusion of the holy period of Ramadan. Our meal included a bread that I recognized from my own culture as a child growing up in Arkansas.

I asked the young lady to talk to me about the bread we were sharing. She explained that it had been prepared by her mother especially for us. I told her that it was very similar to the bread I grew up with, known as hoecakes. For us, it was the last portion of the biscuit dough that could not fit into the pan that went in the oven, so it was cooked atop our stove in one of those cast-iron skillets. I thanked the young lady and asked her to please thank her mother for the wonderful memory it summoned of my own mother, who had recently passed away. We hugged each other as she shed one of those large tears that come from good emotion.

I continue to be amazed at how lives and cultures rhyme in so many ways throughout the world. The great songwriter Curtis Mayfield offered that "People are the same everywhere / They have the same fears / Shed similar tears / Die in so many years." I second that emotion.

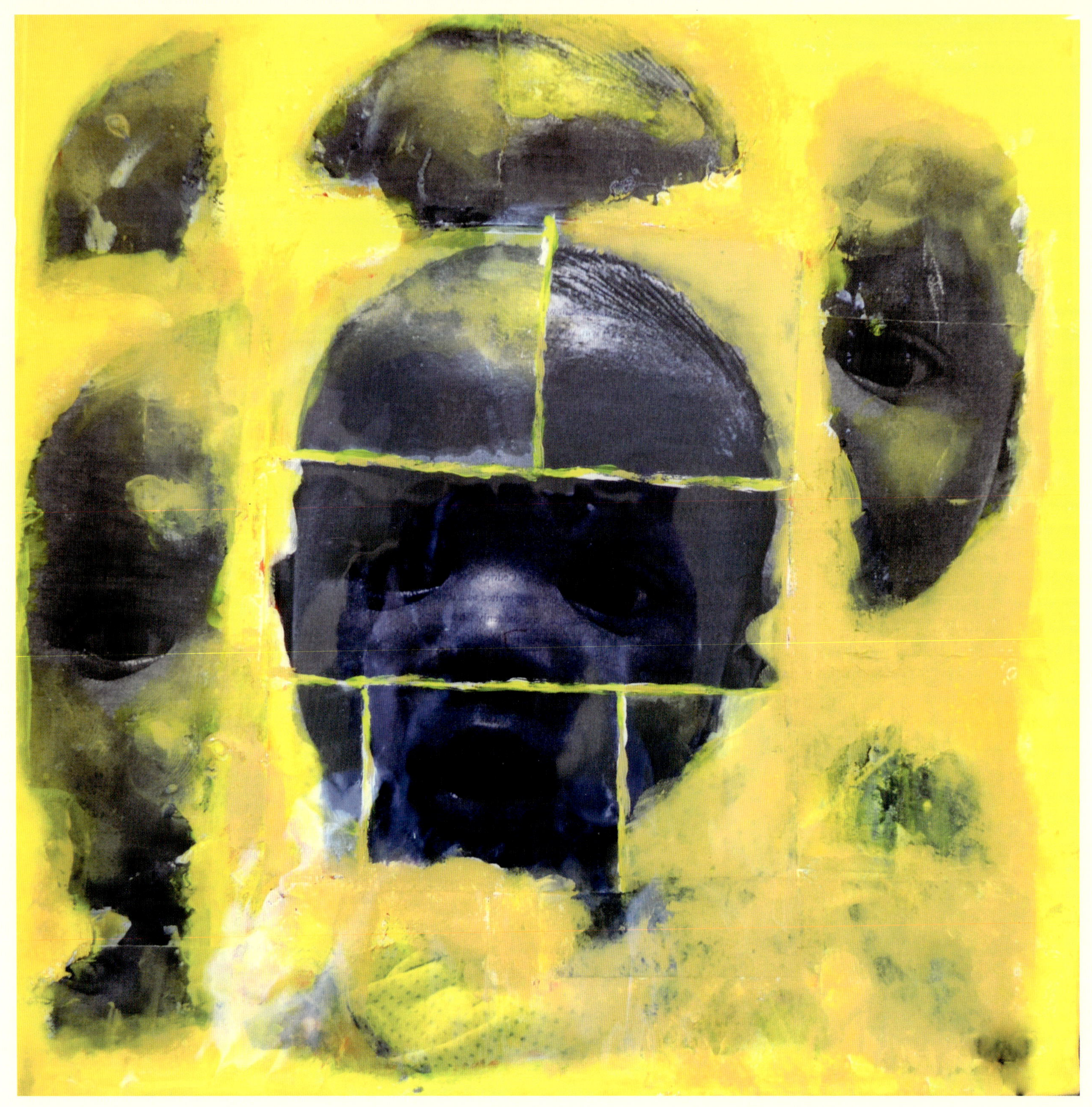

ALPHA

Acrylic and mixed materials on board
14" x 14"

We never know where we are going until we get there…

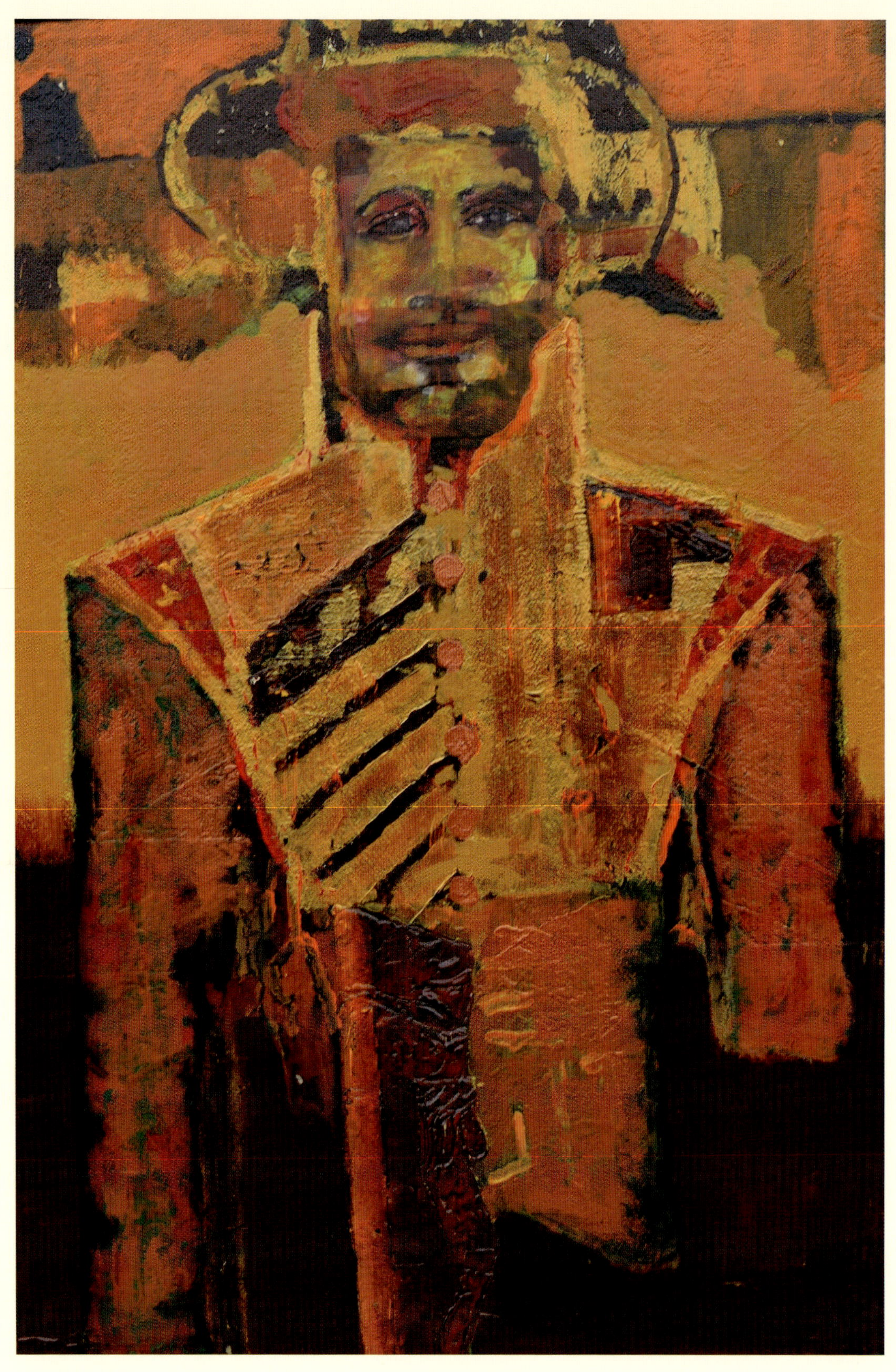

MISTAFRED

Acrylic and mixed materials on board
32" x 48"

AN INTENTION

We grow up expecting so much from life and this world we have inherited. Ambition and enthusiasm have their place. However, as the reality of life creeps in, we are likely to be disappointed proportionately to our expectations. It seems we never recover from the fairy tales we were told early on suggesting that in the end we will be happy, even in the midst of problems, pains, and losses.

Perhaps a time will come when I will have a perfect life. Until that time, I find comfort in laughter, good health, delighting in what is beautiful, enjoying my favorite foods, being present in the moment, giving love, and receiving love in return.

Photography: Joe Barry Carroll

Paintings: Joe Barry Carroll

Consultant: Tara Coyt

Managing Editor: Tara Coyt

Proofreader: Dylan Garity

Cover Art: Joe Barry Carroll

Cover Design: Madison Lux

Layout & Design: Madison Lux

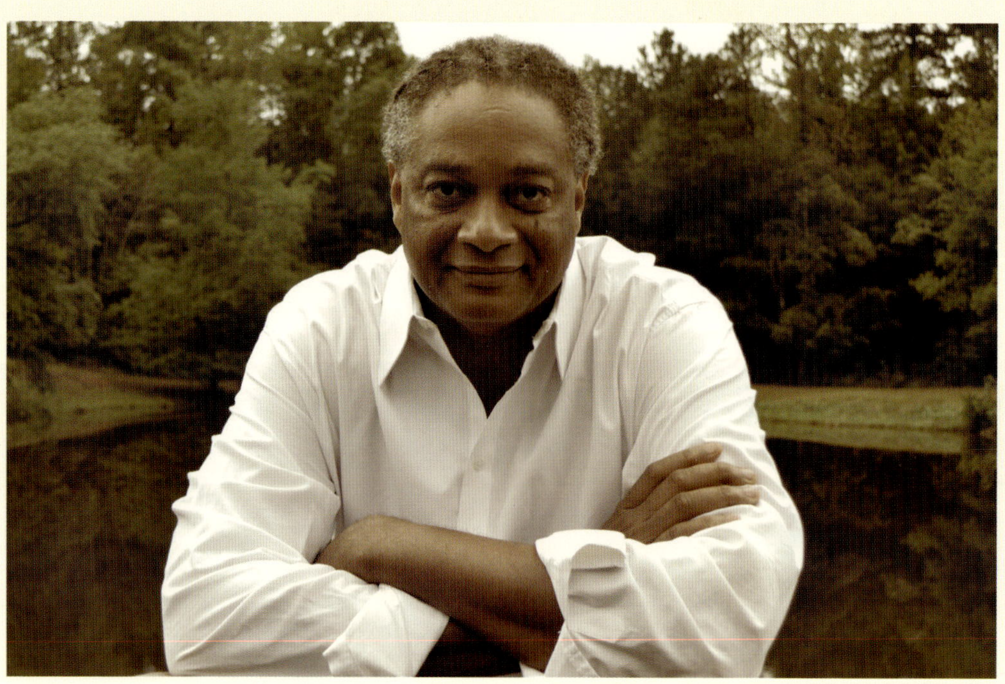

Following an eleven-year professional basketball career, Joe Barry Carroll has explored other talents. The NBA All-Star became a wealth advisor to professional athletes, a philanthropist, artist, publisher, and an award-winning author.

My View From Seven Feet is Carroll's third book. In 2018 Carroll released his second book, *Black American Voices: Shared Culture, Values, and Emotions.* The book is an uplifting collection of narratives, stunning photographs of black Americans, and images of African art from the Zamora Collection, of which he is the trustee. His first publication, *Growing Up . . . In Words and Images* is a memoir coffee-table book. *Growing Up* has been praised for Carroll's southern-comfort prose, memorable stories, and his folk and impressionistic paintings. He has twice been featured at the Arkansas Literary Festival, the Decatur Book Festival, and Roswell Roots.

Joe Barry Carroll graduated from Purdue University with a degree in Economics, was selected NCAA All-American First Team, and led the Purdue Boilermakers to the Final Four in 1980. Soon after, Carroll became the first overall NBA draft pick. He played professional basketball for eleven years with the Golden State Warriors, Milan, Italy, Houston Rockets, New Jersey Nets, Denver Nuggets, and Phoenix Suns. His NBA totals are 12,455 points, 5,404 rebounds, 1,264 assists, 1,122 blocked shots, and a career high average of 24 points in the 1983–84 basketball season.

In 1985 Carroll established BroadView Foundation, a nonprofit to support poor students, communities of color, and other nonprofit organizations. He has committed proceeds from book sales to fund Georgia Innocence Project, public television and radio, American Civil Liberties Union, Repairers of the Breach, and other nonprofit entities. Carroll has also served on boards for the Museum of Contemporary Art, Atlanta and Fulton County Housing Authority. He currently resides in Atlanta, Georgia.